Seduced by metaphor

Seduced by metaphor

Timothy Pilgrim
collected published poems

Cairn Shadow Press
Bellingham, Washington
2021

Each poem in this collection of published poems is a totally creative work and finds its origin in the imagination of Timothy Pilgrim. Except for inspiration or phrasal seed from a person indicated below a poem title in parentheses, any resemblance to actual events, locales, organizations, or persons, living or dead, is entirely coincidental.

Copyright 2021 by Timothy Pilgrim

Rights of all poems in this collection have reverted from the original publisher to Timothy Pilgrim and are reserved. Acknowledgment of the initial publisher is indicated at the end of each poem. No part of this publication may be reproduced, stored in a retrieval system, or transmitted in any form or means, electronic, mechanical, photocopying, recording or otherwise, without prior written permission by the author.

ISBN: 978-1-7341352-4-4
Library of Congress Control Number: Pending

Cairn Shadow Press
Seduced by metaphor:
Timothy Pilgrim collected published poems
First printing, March 2021
Second printing, October 2021

Contact: CairnShadowPress@gmail.com
Cover photo, Montana Pioneer Mountains storm: Carolyn J. Dale;
Pilgrim portrait: Eugene Dale; Pilgrim on horse: Lola Huxtable

Find all Pilgrim's poetry at
www.timothypilgrim.org

Printed in the United States of America
Cairn Shadow Press
Bellingham, Wash. 98225

Acknowledgments

This book of poems could not have come to fruition without the help and inspiration of friends and family.

Most importantly, I am deeply indebted to novelist and short story writer Carolyn Dale, also my wife, who has inspired many poems and has been my primary sounding board for all but forty of the hundreds of published poems in this volume.

Thanks also to fellow poets Paul Piper and Chuck Luckmann — who have critiqued a great many of the poems as part of a poetry writing group Luckmann started over 20 years ago — and to friends Paul Baier, Dan Breeden, Nejat Hulusi, Tom Husby and Sarah McLain, who have inspired me over the years.

Another Montana native and longtime friend, Glen Larum, now a Texas novelist (***Waltz Against the Sky***), poet (***Leaving Montana***) and memoir writer (***A Longtime Gone***), has read many poems and offered wonderful criticism.

Ideas and inspiration also came from Bellingham friends such as Luther Allen, Judy Kleinberg, Steve Giordano, Lynn Rosen, Anna Eblen, Rick Popish, Sarah Brownsberger and Hafthor Yngvason, and from colleagues during my years teaching at Western Washington University in Bellingham, such as Gary McKinney, Jennifer Keller, Maria McLeod, Stephen Howie, Dean Wright, and Bill O'Neill.

Years ago, too, I was influenced at the University of Montana by poets Richard Hugo and James Welch, and by professor Lois Welch, and later at the University of Washington by poet Nelson Bentley and fellow poetry students such as Nancy Bartley and Stephen Quig.

Inspiration has come, too, from my daughter Kamie and son John, daughter-in-law Tammy, grandchildren Cross, Wyley and Symone, and those who are like my own children: Todd DePuy, Helen DePuy, Kezia DePuy Zito, Traci Case, and especially Alex Vouri, whose wonderful way to turn a phrase gave me ideas for many poems and poem titles.

And, needless to say, I am extremely grateful to all the publications who accepted my poems.

Timothy Pilgrim
January 2021

Contents

Acknowledgments, *v*

Introduction, *ix*

A Pilgrim in his own wright, page 1
    Poems, 2020 page 3
    Poems, 2019 page 33
    Poems, 2018 page 59
    Poems, 2017 page 91
    Poems, 2016 page 131
    Poems, 2015 page 167
    Poems, 2014 page 193

Part professor, part poet, page 219
    Poems, 2013 page 221
    Poems, 2012 page 245
    Poems, 2011 page 273
    Poems, 2010 page 309
    Poems, 2000-09 page 333

Early Pilgrim, reluctant cowboy, page 361
    Poems, 1990-99 page 363
    Poems, 1980-89 page 379
    Poems, pre-1980 page 401
    Pilgrim's first poem page 409

Index of poem titles, page 411

About the author, page 417

Introduction

Seduced by metaphor (title poem first published by **Jeopardy Magazine** in 1998) is a collection of all Timothy Pilgrim's published poems — presented in *reverse chronological order.*

Pilgrim lived his first 28 years in Montana and taught high school there before leaving to teach college, almost entirely in the Pacific Northwest. Family and friends know him as sensitive and funny, and he has always been a man of practical abilities who cherished outdoor experiences, run races and marathons, and in the past decade made yoga a daily part of his life.

And, for nearly his entire life, he has been visited by muses and compelled to write.

Pilgrim has lived primarily in the Pacific Northwest, the last 28 in Bellingham, Wash., where he married Carolyn Dale, a journalism department colleague and, now, a retired college professor.

The numbers

This collection begins with poems published or accepted in 2020 and is divided into three major parts:

- **A Pilgrim in his own wright**, recent poetry presented by year (2020, 2019, 2018, etc. through 2014);
- **Part professor, part poet**, presented in five sections (2013, 2012, 2011, 2010, 2000-09); and
- **Early Pilgrim, reluctant cowboy**, offered in three sections (1990-99, 1980-89, and pre-1980).

As of fall 2020, 497 Pilgrim poems had been accepted by 107 different publications: literary and other journals, anthologies, books of contest winners, newspapers, and other publications, such as newsletters, environmental publications — and even his grade-school booklet about his life.

Of course, 497 does not mean 497 *different* poems but, instead, 497 different acceptances. Some poems have been published by several different publications.

For example, "Breathing snow," which uses an avalanche as a metaphor for a relationship's end, has been published eight times, first in 2013 by **Sue Boynton Poetry Contest** and later that year by **Thick With Conviction**.

It was then included in 2014 in ***Bellingham Poems***, a collection published by Flying Trout Press, and a year later in a five-year collection of Boynton winners — and again in 2016 in Pilgrim's first book of poems, ***Mapping water***.

The poem was later republished in 2017 in **Poetry Pacific**, in 2019 by **Better Than Starbucks,** and again early in 2020 in the **River Poets Journal** seasonal issue.

But "Breathing snow" is not in this collection eight times, instead only once — in the year it first appeared.

A few poems have been accepted but not published. For example, after University of Washington poet Nelson Bentley, who was Pilgrim's poetry teacher and one of his mentors, died in 1989, the **Seattle Review**, which Bentley had edited, accepted "Instrument of surrender: Breaking it off at the Little Bighorn battlefield."

Interim editor Steve Quig was drawn to the poem and accepted it, but said in an interview that when the journal's staff changed, the poem somehow got overlooked and was never printed.

Pilgrim believes a poem is never *final*, and many of the poems here have been polished or have small revisions since they were accepted. (This is indicated in the credit line beneath a poem that would read *earlier version published by blank journal*.) Also, Pilgrim took the liberty of changing stanza divisions in some poems here to enhance the book's layout.

Pilgrim's publication record can be likened to a small snowball being rolled into a large one — one poem published every year or two, then several poems each year and, finally, several dozen poems annually.

Pilgrim was busy living life at the bottom of Mazlow's hierarchy (at levels focused on physiological needs like food and rest) from the 1970s until he retired in mid-2013 as emeritus associate professor of journalism at Western Washington University.

Thus, his early publication record is sporadic because he devoted most of his time to preparing for class and grading papers, and because he lacked sufficient time to do the extra work of typing cover letters, preparing the self-addressed envelopes, trekking to the post office, and purchasing required stamps for return postage before mailing out submissions.

The electronic communications age set poets everywhere free, and Pilgrim began to submit more and more poems — and to receive more and more acceptances. For example, in 2011 alone, he had 42 poems accepted (in 21 different journals and other publications), about the same number as were accepted in his first 40 poetry-publishing years.

His yearly acceptances increased after retirement. Between 2014 and late-2020, he published about 300 poems, an average of one poem about every 12 days.

(Of course, his rejections increased in those years as well — by the time of this collection, he was receiving "sincere regrets" an average of once every three days.)

The grit

Seduced by metaphor's title poem suggests a love affair with creative language and evokes the spirit of Pilgrim's Montana roots, resulting in poems replete with memories mixed with dreams.

In reading this volume (where by alphabetical accident, the first poem he published — in his own sixth-grade booklet — is the last poem in the book), one discovers the wide range of muses visiting Pilgrim during his Montana years, and after.

However, he has long insisted almost all his work has a snippet of something more: a bit of hope flitting ceremonially through every poem written or waiting to be imagined.

A glimpse of this appears within each of the aspects of life he has explored:

He offers poems about his parents (deceased), and daughter and son, and friends, living and gone — for example, "Exhalation" (mother), "Hear no evil," "Erasing black," (father), "Birches: the father seeks absolution" (daughter) and "My only son" and "Pre-dawn vigil at the Kootenai Medical Center" (son).

He writes about love's kindling, flaming and extinguishing — for example, "Seduced by metaphor," along with "Destined to rhyme," "Angle of repose," "Reprise for hope," "Still glow," "Instrument of surrender" "Tent not taken" and "Richter Scale."

He also explores the heat and desire of physical love — for example, "Storm," "Chicken," "Bakery," "Cairn," "Hot" and "Primary love, complementary colors."

His poems are often philosophical — for example, "Existential haircut," "Late call from Plato's cave," "When I went out to hang myself," "If God searches your room," "Gravity of the situation," and "The end."

Like the poet Richard Hugo, whom he knew in the early '70s at the University of Montana, he values "triggering towns" and finds inspiration in them and many similarly triggering scenic places — for example, "Out of Missoula," "Still the only bar in Dixon, Montana," "Martha's Cafe," "At White House Ruins," "Ketchum, Idaho: At the Hemingway Memorial," "Working with wind at Canyon de Chelly," "La Push" and "Homecoming to Dungeness Spit."

He is passionate about the Earth's predicament — for example, "To Exxon," "No more argument," "Slick — to Exxon then and BP now," "Sea change," "Bituminous nightmare," "Solstice ceremony at Medicine-walker's," "Gestapo glaciers," "Last," "Final blizzard," and "No more robbery."

He finds significance in science and imaginatively explores its findings — for example, "The hum," "Light found to have weight," "Higgs-Boson particle," "Vast silence," "Going south," "Quid pro quo," and "Covert rainbow."

He believes in social justice, and many poems advocate for it and speak of racism, sexism and the harm done to First Nations — for example, "At the White Supremacist cross burning," "In which he accepts the feminist point of view," "God walks out of math proficiency exam," "Laminated," "Vast silence," "Homeless night watchman," "Redemption," "Belly up," and "At the Nez Perce camp with Spirit Woman."

He has a history of poems deploring violent masculinity — for example, "Fitting end," "Violent male rut," "Let us dream," "Two dogs, one stick," "Like a fenced-in dog," and "Final say."

He has long been a critic of war and America's reveling in all things military — for example, "This being America, there were patriots present," "Afghanistan misery index," "War memorial," "Tending nuclear bombs," "Breathing lesson," "All quiet on the Iraqi front," and "Long stumps of hope."

His poems may examine religion and sometimes dissect it — for example, "Hawking holy books," "Texting the savior," "Resigning from being messiah," "The lord's tweet," "Second Coming expert," and "Topless woman steals baby Jesus from Vatican nativity scene."

He immensely enjoys language and word play and loves to turn, twist and rip a phrase — for example, "Plotting shadows from the chaos," "Existential diagram," "Déjà vu tridundancy," "Powdered water," "Parenthetical," "Gerunds running down my leg," "Things are well and going good," and "Diagramming love."

He dabbles in the style used by other poets, sometimes teasingly — for example, "My last professor" (after Robert Browning), "My mama's waltz" (after Theodore Roethke), "The heaped wheelbarrow" (after William Carlos Williams), "Headboard" (after Malinda Finney Briggs), and "I herded flies, Buzz, when I dyed" (after Emily Dickinson).

He is sometimes unkind to the pretentious, be it in poetry, academia or politics — for example, "Reading," "Screw the pretentious poets," "Question of humility," "Lit exam," "Old poet," "Publishing in The New Yorker," "Etiquette lesson," and "Executive orders."

But he is also drawn to humor and, perhaps too often or too obscurely, ladles it into his poems — for example, "Conspiracy of vegetarians," "Vacuuming your cat," "The capes we wear," "Almost," or "Pawnshop."

Or, "Death by chocolate," "Gettysburg tweet," "Traitor Joe," "Dashboard savior," "Side effects may include," "Ken Burns Effect," "Posse of angels," "Student loan repayment time," and "Wrong a lot."

Yet, throughout almost all his poetry, that glimmer of hope can be seen. In offering this volume, Pilgrim regrets that poems not yet accepted — for example, "Binge novel," "Black swirls," "Upon my arrival," "Pray, Montana," "Crossing," and "Winding up winding down" — cannot be included, nor new poems and those yet to be imagined and written.

But, he promises to keep all of these available on his poetry website (www.timothypilgrim.org), as well as his published poems, each of which is paired with a photo or photo-illustration, and if the *cloud* does not rain, will be accessible for weeks, and, with luck, maybe even years to come.

A Pilgrim in his own wright

Poems arranged alphabetically by year:

    2020 pages 3-32
    2019 pages 33-58
    2018 pages 59-90
    2017 pages 91-130
    2016 pages 131-166
    2015 pages 167-192
    2014 pages 193-218

Poems 2020

A few obscene words escape

my mouth, not to mention,
a wounded sparrow of despair

flying out of my soul
as I watch her drive away,

the whole thermos of mimosas
nestled between her thighs,

warm brioche with cherry filling
lying on the seat beside.

    (published by **Gold Man Review**)

Antique store mannequin

First glance, I believe it's you
doing a headstand, offering
my way back in. Inverted eyes,

green, bright, avoid mine, stare
at tires, hubcaps, wrenches, rims.
Legs slightly spread rise taut,

stilettoed heels stab ceiling lights.
Black stockings re-stir the urge —
somehow skirt security lock,

help shoes, nylons, panties off.
The dream must pass. You packed,
clicked out the door, chose condo,

mate, golden Porsche. No chance
for me or antique store, you
trapped, windowed, upside-thighed,

winking, inviting millennial guys,
hey, you, come in, spend time,
browse fine junk, don't pass by.

    (published by **Spindrift**)

At the Vietnam War Memorial

Aged. Going down, gutted. Again.
More and more names.
Anderson, Andrews.

Archer — stole my girl, died
in some dark tunnel. Hate,
too high a price. Fingers

trace names, memory glazes over.
Black granite reflects my life,
ghostlike history now a haze,

enemies and friends,
like Archer, remembered — war
out of mind. So many to recall.

Soon, one final reflection, mine,
on stone. It's definitely me, us,
U.S., I don't believe, trust.

    (published by **Otoliths**)

Blueprint

In the end, they did not have time to club
every protester in body armor of adobe,

nor those unclothed, tattooed all over
with sledge hammers inked black.

City police, precincts demolished long ago,
now worked without papers in the kitchen.

Clueless as to what was building,
federal agents quarreled over takeout

at Taco Bell. Sheetrock, ever racist,
cowered at Lowe's in white piles, livid.

(published by **The Bond Street Review**)

The capes we wear

Superman tattooed on one arm,
Batman taking up the other,

original Wonder Woman on thigh,
you leave her, heinous, behind,

steer for Montana, last best place
to escape. Wine in cooler, extra capes

in the trunk, you hum *I'd do anything
for love (but I won't do that)*,

reach Missoula, Sula, Lost Trail Pass.
You batmobile hard into the Big Hole,

keep sharp lookout for evil in cutoffs.
Wisdom is a speck in the distance.

> (published by **Mad Swirl**; republished in 2021
> in ***Best of Mad Swirl: 2020***)

Covert rainbow

Light's not lithe, scientists found —
it has weight. Now they say
time, long known to be a property

of gravity, also packs pounds.
This knowledge giddies me,
I daydream a rainbow

so voluptuous, so heavy
her sides billow, spill from the sky.
Red, green, indigo mix together,

splash down at both ends. Bluebirds
find gold worms, fill backpacks
with them, fly south early,

retire. I am hired as a janitor,
get paid double overtime,
work all night, clean up the mess.

(published by **Mad Swirl**)

Eclectic suitcase

Masked, virus to flee, hurried pack
for flight back, laundry flung

into any bag. My socks, jeans, briefs,
your dresses, skirts, undies,

bras. Totally inconsiderate, teddies,
shirts in one wad. A thousand years

from now — confusion.
Archaeologists at plane-crash dig,

sifting boxers, panties, tees,
perplexed at what it could mean.

    (published by **Otoliths**)

Embers

*Lost love's the Nooksack, winter,
barely flows*, she says then goes.

My fuchsia future lies ahead,
signals loss around the bend —

somewhere beyond pause, yield,
stop, hold breath. More like ice, crack,

splash. Even campfires succumb
to snow, a branch load, fade

from bright to glow. Become
embers, give off scarlet warning

heat must go. Like sun hung
in still sky, low in the west, I cling

to red, desperate not to plunge
over night's black edge.

    (published by **Whatcom Watch**)

Evading gray

I am undone, so is love, the fringe
won't hold. I abandon coast, home,

head for Montana, new chance to be.
Missoula, crossroads, I choose south,

comes dry river, barren stream.
Finally Bannack, half caved in,

stories here, lessons from the past —
like hunter vanished in prairie sage,

gray blanket cloaking paths miners took
to claims, hope sparkling in clumps

of clay. Maybe I stumble on the gold,
gather crazed, get lost, perish

from greed. Or, Plummer's stolen loot —
folks hanged the outlaw sheriff,

no trading noose for secret cache.
I haul it away, choose warm beach,

sun, sea. Perhaps, a hidden shaft,
I fall, climb free, broken, weak.

Gaze west, believe I see the Sound,
die, never get found. I must begin

to breathe, deep, wipe out despair.
Realize Bannack shacks rot,

outsiders, like me, get whipped
by bad wind. Dust always blows in,

buries broken lives, sage, regrets.
The one street here still flees at both ends,

gives the hopeless a chance to leave.
Only the remains will fade to gray.

    (published in **Whatcom Writes Anthology**)

Getting even
(with a nod to Anna Eblen)

Time to end climate debate.
Put snails, slugs to use —
revenge for chewed marigold,

iris, tulip, rose, anything else
green that grows. Creative payback
for half-eaten beans, grape leaves,

arugula, chard, peas. Toss each
in pail, swish them slimeless,
rinse clean. Next-door denier —

his second sin, Fox News
spewed loud at night — text him,
come, argue world's end.

Offer Breadfarm loaf, or two,
non-GMO. Brie, aperitif, Pernod.
A neighborly pile of escargot.

  (published by **Whatcom Watch**)

La chanson

Stir red coals, poke Deer Island beach fire,
again, fiercely. Begin to see
nothing brings back a loving smile —
the mere sight of you cues contempt,

urge to leave. Hang your head,
wish it were your life dropped
in Biloxi Bay waves — despair,
a muffled gong smothered by night.

Time to drown ancient dream —
battle strong surf, pull her to shore,
deep kiss, revived, heated,
straining upward, she breathes.

Like Calypso, she has severed ties,
unraveled knotted love, muted
siren call once tying her to you.
She likely dresses in black, prowls

a far beach, piles photos, poems,
memories of you, sets them ablaze.
Drinks red wine at dusk, fakes
a bit of mourning beside her pyre.

She will scan horizon, sing la chanson
into darkness. Out on the Gulf,
a new Odysseus will hear, lift head,
not know enough to scream.

(published by **San Pedro River Review**)

Last

I

Basement turned swamp,
floor rotted, john flushed up.

Sawgrass out back drooped,
died. Coffins once cemeteried

rose with the tide, floated
dead bones by. Sopped clothes

packed, *this house, free*,
painted on porch turned raft,

I fled Florida for new home.
High bluff, Vancouver coast,

sweeping view — oil trains,
tankers, black smoke.

II

Gulf risen, gone east
to greet Biscayne Bay,

deniers dog-paddled there,
trapped, squeezed,

contained. They tweeted,
texted, blogged,

played with their phones.
Ate seaweed, dreamed

it was filleted, creped, creamed.
The last were the last

to drown — even the aftermath
steered clear, still went down.

    (published by **Soliloquies Anthology**)

Last one clapping

Applaud longer than anyone else —
viable goal to achieve. Uber success,

no app needed, nothing left
to chance. Screw elusive dreams,

greatness promised later — president,
rock star, sex after the prom,

beauty queen. Winner, lottery,
spelling bee, Nobel Prize for peace.

    (published by **Mad Swirl**)

Let us dream

for one day, no shootings, not five,
not eight. No teen blogging hate,
no deranged shooter taking aim,
no macho guy firing away.

Let us dream
someday we see it's always males —
violent boys, violent men — back then,
muskets, carbines, Colts, today,
Berettas, Glocks, Heckler & Koch.

Let us dream
we begin to see women suffer
most of the rage, cower, shake —
tough guys shooting lovers, wives,
other men, strangers, friends.

Let us dream
culture finds a way to change —
men stop blasting black, brown, red,
come home to rest — for fun,
shoot rabbits, ravens, robins, wrens.

Let us dream
we expunge the urge to kill — drones,
bombs go away, male violence becomes
public health threat number one.
Finally, we learn how not to prey.

    (earlier version published by **Howl**)

Man pleads guilty in death of relationship

She said goodness may lie within me,
even praised my gentle ways.
Her brother agreed, later confided
he wanted to kill me,

not that I would stop him,
choke off his Iraq-aholic dreams,
refuse to convulse on desert floor,
Rorschached maroon, death being

a mailman with bad news,
no one in search of letters,
always at a distance,
ignoring mail-call snarl,

it's for you.
We all kill something —
by accident mostly —
smother it, then ourselves,

with guilt, even as we invite
our postal carrier in at Christmas,
serve up a shriveled fruitcake,
say, *take rum-soaked bread chunked red,*

have a hot toddy for your time.
She suffered, knew I am no warrior,
forgave mistakes, cut sand-blown ties,
absolved anemic love webbed in by life.

So I lie alone, wallow wounded —
no wonder clerks fake headaches
to avoid me in their line,
why I blocked her out, all her needs,

why self-pity whets my appetite.
I dream myself a Tigris killer,
move ghost-like through the streets.
I wear polyester, not fatigues.

   (published by **Jeopardy**)

My conclusive dance frame

rigid, classic, like parentheses
trapping a flutter of sparrows

mid-theft, chicken coop, after grain.
No match for hers, corseted tight,

white-laced, as she denied my bid
to diagram our pas de deux

across the ballroom floor. A feud,
two stern teachers, each certain —

how to construct the perfect sentence,
our grammar book of would-be love,

unbound, sections lying random
among whirling couples, the chapter

beneath us, ironically, open to rules
on passive voice, page thirty-three.

(published by **Mad Swirl**)

New twist on the end

Captive to an explosion happening,
each spark hitching a fling into blackness,
the light beside dazzled shadows

with shine and glow. Fire that had burned
at the core, a genesis of sorts,
streaked behind into universal night.

It would eventually pockmark time.
One trace remained, a fuse of coiled rope,
still embered, writhing on the tile floor.

   (published by **Mad Swirl)**

Obsession

Tear off price tag,
Behind the Glamour $18,

next to long row, prison-cell lines,
crush bar code into a tight ball,

toss it away. The wad won't let go,
adheres to fingers, as if to chide,

Marilyn's worth any price.
Study her photos by the bed,

wonder if Prufrockean meaning
lies in stickiness, steamy novels,

all those Norma Jean YouTube posts.
Probably not, given white sheets,

imagined whisper, throaty, low,
Must flee white men using me.

    (published by **Otoliths**)

Old poet

I find it in The New Yorker now
easier to yawn about nothing poems —

self-obsessed men, depression, sanity
on the run, priests preying on nuns.

Phallic prayer naked, life, spread wide
for redemption, full bosomed end.

So little depends on anything
when limp metaphors droop and bend.

    (published by **Toasted Cheese**)

Recalling fragments

of a poem flitting off,
say, about a life breaking apart,

like a sensitive, fragile universe,
pieces flying off dark

after colliding with another universe —

a voluptuous, curvy one,
low-throat purr, unfaithful,

ready to leave on a whim,
selfish, full of black holes.

    (published by **The Bond Street Review**)

Runner-up disciple

Like America, Justus, next in line
but outside — apart. Almost a part.

Just us, we two, screw you.
A good man, well, maybe heavy

on greed, lust, just not good enough.
Of ninety apostles, fill Judas' spot,

one rule — no more betrayal,
but don't forget about race.

Justus did not seal deal, seize
victory, cheat to win, build a wall.

Matthias takes the robe, makes it
an even dozen again. Runner-up

done in by Twitter, tweet, eyelash,
Jesus winking from the shadows.

Irony nailed to humility.
The payback, blind justice for all.

(published by **Otoliths**)

Solstice ceremony at Medicine-walker's
(with a nod to Rainbow Medicine-walker)

Rainbow strokes drum again,
beat probing bonfire flame,

invoking Mother Earth, water, air.
She summons power, the ancients,

an unkindness of ravens, lets go
a murder of crows. Day, on the fade,

dips red, lilac, pink, finds gray.
We circle the blaze — whirl, dance,

chant. Sparks snap, rise bright,
take flight with our prayers, clear

cedar trees, high. My hope for them —
surge deep into cringing night.

   (published by **Otoliths**)

Solstice ceremony near Mount Baker

Nooksack River flows by black,
drums intensify in fading light,
inspire bonfire, Earth, air, new life.

We circle the blaze, dance, chant,
summon an unkindness of ravens,
ancient power. I see Spirit Woman

float in from shadows, offer
feathers, berries, salmon strips —
place the oblation in quieted flames.

We add boughs, urge fire, revive.
Sparks gather our prayers, clear pine,
fir, cedar trees. The spatter brightens,

pierces night, floats off east.

(published by **Whatcom Watch**)

Spiral down

Taught to dream yourself popular,
at the prom, crowned queen.

Another good-hair day, makeup,
perfect, white gown, chiffon.

You dance every dance,
king never grabs your ass,

cuts you off. Your selfies
go viral, Twitter groupies

retweet, praise. Dreams fade —
you wake, MeToo life in place.

Hair, flat, skin broken out,
prom dress turned nightgown.

Your cell phone, dead,
Facebook life spiraled down.

    (earlier version published by **Howl**)

Text from the exotic pets store

Ants farming here gather for the service,
bury their dead near the edge,
return to work. They ignore the light,

dig new passages in old sand,
carry a thousand times their weight,
eat, sleep. Two may antennae, touch,

tap out a brief embrace, make ways past,
take separate tunnels — not marry,
grow apart, escape. Forgive me, love,

I babble on. Just texting to say
mistake I left, only hours away.
Put on music, light the candles,

open red wine, let it breathe. Don't call —
if the key still works, I'll let myself in,
we'll dance all night in the hall.

(published by **Tipton Poetry Journal**)

Topless woman steals baby Jesus from Vatican nativity scene
(with a nod to Euronews.com)

Carried carved infant to a boat,
floated down the Tiber, him safe
in valley between her breasts.

Shouted her maiden name
was Dante, at Christmas missed
nine levels of hell, also Les Baux.

Said she alone dared save
the savior. The Pope viewed
surveillance video many times,

decreed Jesus could not return —
a plastic one must fill the role.
Her lawyer focused on fear —

alleged priests made threats, stole
her clothes. She had to promise
never to row to shore for more.

    (published by **Burnt Pine**)

Violent male rut

Same blue sky frames recurrent clouds,
one more sun, boring gold, shines round.

Birds head home, homogenous tree,
re-fluff, beak déjà vu repeated tweets.

I walk my normal trail, joggers —
always guys — again slog by, snarl

in unison another *hi*. Repeat yesterday,
bring out Glocks, take aim, spray

a dozen school-bound kids. They yawn,
put smoking guns away — consider it

repetitious slay. I speed-dial 911, report
the deed. A cop car re-runs over me.

    (published by **Howl**)

Viral ending

Lifted masks, brief kiss, on the lips.
Turned away, skipped some stones,

she went to tinkle (feel free to call it
urinate or pee). Once out of sight,

doubled back. I Purelled, waited,
dreamed, paced like a cat. She packed,

emptied my place. Took can opener,
tuna tins, T-paper, stopper for the sink.

Left bleach, vacuum, blue vinyl gloves,
stale bag of Lays, litter box to clean.

(published by **Mad Swirl**)

Wash your hands

after, and before,
you go. With this virus, rinse away

the desire to touch everything hugged,
grabbed, stroked by roving hand.

Wipe off dirt, germs, those deeds
long in need of a serious clean.

It's not as if we were paintings
being restored, say, every century

or so — sucked-up dust, lifted grime,
colors, vivid, brought back to life —

nor glaciers on the rise, climate change
un-bona fide, years, decades, scores ago.

Think of it — stranded on roofs, no fever,
no cough, risen sea all around,

the unwashed, certain they'll stay pure,
never be stricken, never sink down.

    (published by **Cirque**)

Poems 2019

America, 2019

Hiking Mexico, northern desert, I saw a wall.
Huge. Tall. Stretching horizon to horizon.

I grabbed a rope ladder from my backpack,
crouched, flung it high — it caught the edge.

I climbed up, perched on top, looked down.
Human-like creatures ran about, rifles

strapped to backs, pistols holstered below
fat bellies. Heads shaved, they wore sweats

with flag patterns, carried long, serrated knives.
Each was busy cutting open

another's head. They saw me peering
down, stopped, looked up. *Won't you miss*

your brains? I asked. *What?* they shouted,
then skipped off together, free.

>   (published by **Cascadia Weekly**; adapted
>   from Pilgrim's poem, "This being America,
>   there were patriots present," published
>   in 2010 by **The Curious Record**)

Bible tweet

To begin
God made it all
U no — Eve snake
Moses laws Ark
manger Jesus preach
teach Judas
cross up he goes
to clean mansions
he'll be back

    (published by **Mad Swirl**)

Brautigan breakfast

Cabin, deep mountain woods,
dawn squatting, dripping dew,

I rise, light fire, blow coals
red. You put on coffee, grease

the pan, creep, lithe, a doe
salt-licked, back to bed.

Skillet sizzles fried spuds —
famished, so does love.

    (published by **Cascadia Rising Review**)

Déjà-vu tridundancy

Look back — at you, silent,
quiet on path, peering behind

as sun lights forest — trees,
groved, rooted, branched.

Meadow before, open expanse,
grassy, wide, vast. Stream, still,

wending, twisted brook, placid.
Creek, glassy, sinuous, flat.

Banks, all spongy, soft, dank.
Listen closely, strain to hear

inner voice — soft query, whisper
to yourself, question murmured

where you're going, headed, bound.
Déjà-vu etiquette forbids reply,

response, re-ask. Amid pine, cedar,
tamarack, be still, looking back.

>   (earlier version published by **Adelaide
>   Independent Monthly Literary Magazine**)

Dream back
(for Cheryl)

Cheeks red with hives, alone
in bed, she knows she's fucked,
turns away, cries. She hopes

doctors won't steal her spirit
as they drain fluid from lungs,
inject six drugs to poison

ten tumors taking over
what's left of her brain.
Allow strength to leave pain

behind, soak in morning sun,
hike the Cascades. Pitch tent,
build fire, in moonlight

sit astride lover, dream back
bear lily, paintbrush, lupine.
Wake to lightning, run naked,

spin. Lift head tearless, face
raw wind. Spread arms, lift chin,
embrace the coming storm.

(published by **Panoplyzine**)

Fake nudes

Cuckold, empty, luckless, lost,
I fear the worst — curse lack
of courage, moxie, verve.

Skirt museum, opt for thrift store
two doors down. Pass clothes,
pots, armoires, lamps, find

statues way in back — naked man,
ancient, nothing hanging low to note.
Phone tight in hand, scowl etched

on face, jowls, belly spewing fat.
Lady, undraped too, doughy breasts,
sutured, huge. Butt, evidence

of the coming droop. Venus, David
behind, sculpted plastic marble,
smooth. Blow-up Santa, beardless,

nude, plus, a window mannequin,
or two. Perfect place — fake friends,
stained bed. I undress, tuck me in.

(published by **Spindrift**)

Holstered

Lord of tunnels, I am free,
outside. A new man,
no longer in my dark period

of burning stalactites.
I fall in step beside her,
briefly desire to be back

inside, maybe after dinner.
Tonight, rain could mean
moist embers. Of course,

following good cognac
and a buttery dessert.
The black-leather love

she points at me excites
a deep urge to unholster
my shovel filled with volition.

    (published by **Mad Swirl**)

The hum

Secrets lie at the heart of it —
knowledge nestled inside,
not to be let loose, at least

not soon. Humming signals
the secret — musical clue,
elusive, hint to exude,

never a murmur, whisper, song.
Glaciers hum, Antarctica hums.
Wind whips across ice shelf,

disturbs snow, causes movement,
produces a faint hum. Mist
shrouds mountain peaks, fog

bellies along streams, crawls
into valleys, obscures fir,
tamarack, spring. Wind scuds

across scree, past boulders,
over cairns. If we hold breath,
listen, intent, the hum is clear.

Scientists have found all nature
is humming — in F major,
the secret likely a lesson on how

to keep Earth alive. Our secret —
a report card, hidden, for shame.
Grade in humming — F minus.

(published by **Harbinger Asylum**)

Intensely dead

Meadowed, willowed, snaking wide,
I fish a mountain stream,
loop fly through fading sky.
Test riffles on the far, dark side.

No blurred cutthroat splash,
hopeful offering left afloat,
I yield, find tent, snuff light. Dream
life's centered edge won't hold —

lightning strikes my lover,
sleeping spent beside another.
Smoldered, seared, she survives.
Death, no longer a final dip,

the end. Now, afterlife with depth,
degree. Possibility beyond cuckold.
Intensely dead, diving deeper,
fathoms past passed away.

Endless time to fish ebony streams,
re-kindle dying dreams. Rise,
build a morning fire, heap it
high with blackened tears.

(published by **Harbinger Asylum**;
republished by **Cirque**)

It is what it was

Trite after a while, the phrase,
it is what it is. Means no choice,

frozen, stuck. Allows no way
to act on where we've been,

improve the future, give it sense,
spruce it up. Even caged geese,

by accident, beak latch,
open gate, give grass a scratch,

learn to re-beak, escape,
swim, splash. More wise to glance

behind, let the past teach.
It is what it WAS — a mirror beyond

the black. Green light reflected,
ahead, down the road a bit.

    (published by **Otoliths**)

Laminated

Crowded beach, she stretches, yawns,
squirms belly deep into soft sand,
dreams she casts off stifling bikini,

sets breasts free, swims with turtles,
warms the sea. Slug of a guy
leers for a time, bends, whispers,

*Wow, outstanding ass — round, firm,
so fine it should be laminated.*
She smiles, motions him near,

*I totally agree. Imagine — just me,
brown belly, nice tits, great butt,
thick acrylic keeping assholes away.*

(published by **Spindrift**)

La Push

Wend away from Kalaloch, leave miles
of beached cedar logs behind, pass
Ruby Beach, sand there, a gritty cradle

for imagined jewels glittering
in morning sun. Ignore haystack rocks
stretching for sky from Pacific waves

still trying to grind them into powder
after five million years. You have life left,
enough to let such memories fade.

Pass by Hoh River, soggy rainforest
gone moss-insane — two hundred inches
of drizzle tricking huckleberry bushes

into taking root in crook of cedar,
new life fifty feet toward gray sky.
Refuse to be fooled — head north

for Forks. Turn west, make for La Push,
mystic beach, where winds blow through
like a mistral on speed, the pines

bowing down broken in rows of prayer.
Quileute still carve traditional canoes,
totem poles stand here and there

as sentinels waiting for whale-filled boats.
Old canoes decay on the sand,
no tent can remain long, each kited

skyward. Your best bet, the lodge,
no line, check in. Find stairs
to Fifties room half-rotten,

walls, slime green. The curtains,
shredded, each rip a black space
between bony remains of your life.

Sit by the dirty window. Stare
at endless gray before what passes
as anemic sun floats belly up into night.

    (published by **Windfall**)

Love advice

Now is the time to mingle,
just the two of you. Don't let

a minute go by, an hour pass.
Seek the opening, be keen

about entry — intent on it, even.
Yearn for her. Act euphoric,

ardent, blithe. Promise roses,
candy, wine. Shimmer, hover,

make a fuss. Offer a ride.
If she remains distant, aloof, cool,

bring out the big gifts — iPhone,
smart TV, necklace of gold.

Jet ski, Lexus, gossamer drone.
As a last resort, draw and quarter

your heart. Gift-wrap the pieces,
add bows, blue, white —

four throbbing loves, passion
pumped into her gaping life.

    (published by **The Kumquat Poetry Challenge**
    under the title "Last-ditch love plan")

My mama's waltz
(with a nod to Theodore Roethke)

The perfume on your dress
could drive a young boy crazy —
dark lust, secret untold since —
our nightly ritual, flow and bend.

We whirled from room to room,
circled smooth and tight,
each turn, our pas de deux,
much spinning out of sight.

Our dance from dark to light,
my face against your dress,
dizzy with each pass at dusk,
clinging, waiting to be blessed.

Shadows softened at the edge,
his absence not undone,
you waltzed me off to bed,
lonely mother, love-torn son.

>(earlier version published by **Adelaide Independent Monthly Literary Magazine**)

Never wrong

Let's canoe to the island,
more stable than a raft.
I'm certain my girlfriend

hates to dance. Text me
from work, your boss
won't mind. Cut down

the tree, it won't hit
your home. I date
her friend, she'll never know.

I'm really sober, plenty good
to drive. No texts for days,
she must want me back.

It's best to eat steak, salmon
puts on fat. These jeans
are clean, my breath

smells great. Still no text,
she must be depressed.
No need for a coat,

I'll never catch cold.
I prefer to be alone,
am happy she left.

    (published by **Otoliths**)

Out of Montana, for good

Condos rented on the Blackfoot, cabins
up the Swan, outsiders stomp grass
along the wrong river, seldom see
cutthroat glow red, take on brilliance,
flash past a Black Ghost, dive deep,

wait, not feed. They invade taverns,
belly up to bar, drink with locals,
buy good bourbon, beer, boast of SUVs,
past raft trips, their gear. They lie
to pry secrets — how, when, where

to fish. We don't say, *the Bitterroot,
Lolo, Rock Creek, all of them great —
it's not price of rod, line, which fly.
You must think like a fish, creep
silent through tall grass, stay*

*way back. Fish narrow water, cast fly
to lupine on the far bank. Tug,
make it fall helpless, struggle,
float to the riffle — easy prey
for trout undulating in shade.*

We drink their booze, tell them,
*Take the bad fork, follow wide path
through pine. Wear orange, bright red,
lime. Stay near the road, fish
wide, shallow water, stand close.*

Best to arrive at noon, day after
full moon. We hope they do,
whip blue sky, snap off flies, no fish
strike. Lines tangle in brush,
they give up, return to their rigs,

drink, sleep. Dream of Wyoming,
the rainbow there huge, eager to bite.
Montana, forget it, not worth
the time — rivers, all fishless, water,
clear, cold, running too deep.

(published by **Cascadia Rising Review**)

Powdered water

Dream a quenched love,
gambit akin to chess,
poured into a narrow hallway

from some tall glass — a gauntlet,
say. Not gantlet, two lines,
men with sticks beating cuckolds,

lechers, liars running by. Also,
gimlet nearby — tool to glide
inside a pretty package, bore

the hole deep as gimlet eyes
stare back, fuel lust with a luring,
penetrating look. No need really

for lime-laced drink, gimlet,
nothing powdered in it. Yes, gimbal,
keep everything on course,

even, level. Inspire gamut,
range of thirst so complete
no gauntlet, or any rapid-gulp dare,

makes the thirsty beauty weak,
lethargic, miss why granules
can lure a doe to the damp edge,

inspire thirst — strong desire
to lie back, dream a liquid gift,
wetness not powdered stirred in.

(published by **Santa Ana River Review**)

Python

In another Coleridge dream,
my lithe python, eager

to please, slithers off
down the carpool lane.

Glides slow, pays the toll,
takes the proper exit,

finds the store. She buys
chips, cheap beer, dip,

splurges on a Lycra skin.
Hemmed in at rush-hour,

she threads traffic, somehow
arrives home, brew still cold.

We toke, drink, eat all the treats.
I squeeze her tight again.

   (published by **Mad Swirl**)

Reprise, of a sort

Savage wind slaps screen, sash,
glass again. Her memory blows in,

black slash of night,
like slicing open a fish belly,

finding darkened clumps,
once a spleen or bad liver

in some rainbow's life.
I must find a way to surface, fight,

dream myself back, say,
to dusk, a reprise — last light, brief,

flashing low, moon, full, orange
turned gold, not glowering

before she goes. With luck,
I will be hooked downstream,

the end coming from above
though I lie still in tall grass.

(published by **Jeopardy**)

Shame remains

Use a black marker, fester shadows,
call her ugly, scrawl hate on walls.

Dis Me-too deeds, flame-throw
homeless, flip off the brown

from an SUV. Shoot up a mall,
join the Marines, shop for clothes.

Burn her panties after she goes,
call her whore in a Facebook post.

(published by **Mad Swirl**)

To Exxon 30 years later
(after "To Exxon a year later")

Pipeline, tanker began the sadness.
Your legend as robber baron hangs on,
keeps memories of ebony ice alive,

takes us back to frozen tundra
primed with promises even caribou
knew were lies. We still feel pain

receding glaciers can't scrub away.
Recall how we tromped black sand,
piled oil-soaked murres, seals, otters

shoulder-high, set them ablaze.
We collected bald eagles fallen
from slick sky, tossed them, too,

onto the pyre, watched it outshine
endless dusk. Puffins staggered in,
vainly tried to preen, white feathers

matted down. They wobbled
to Prince William Sound, drooped,
drowned. At night we burned ice

to stay warm. Your lawyers slapped
our backs in bars, bought drinks.
The high court, nine sleek crows —

a murder of them — put out of mind
seabirds, over a quarter million,
thousands of otters, hundreds

of seals, whales, all perished,
their kind never again to thrive.
The court believed your tale: *a tragic,*

*terrible event ... one for which ...
(Exxon) has paid dearly.* They found
no reason for a severe fine. Shores

lie bare now, thick oil still oozes
beneath beach rocks. Beach workers,
seabird washers, the Valdez,

all, gone. Skimmers, booms,
the dead, buried deep in black past.
We dream on Arctic nights

lightning strikes, the whole bay
catches fire, flames race to shore,
find you, burn you out of town.

We wake to salted tears and hate,
twin tides coming on schedule
to spread the hidden crude around.

    (published by **Cascadia Rising Review**)

Too willing a Montana martyr

Hidden by sleep, I weave my way
through sage, weathered boyish charm
beaten down like this looping path.

I creep along, silent, with little hope
of finding real love, let alone dying
of it. I keep a sharp lookout

for any bliss overshadowing me
like an ominous noose. If I do hang,
it will likely be from sadness, say,

in Bannack, next to Plummer,
outlaw sheriff — his gold, vanished
like a faithless lover. As always,

I wake before dawn, watch her breathe,
certainly say nothing erudite
before her first cup of coffee.

>(earlier version published
> by **San Pedro River Review**)

Wild and scenic aneurysm

Love dies like a river — slows, ceases
to flow, she says, tearless, then goes.
My fuchsia future lies ahead,

signals loss around the bend,
beyond swallow, breath, stop, hold —
like a waterfall gone dry, nothing

wet below. Even campfires fade
to glow, become timid embers,
give off a scarlet warning — black

follows gray. Sullen sun, hung low
in the sky, clings to red,
plunges over night's black edge.

> (published by **Whatcom Watch;**
> different version, "Embers," published
> in 2020 by **Whatcom Watch**)

Poems 2018

After the kill

Yes, Alpha, you ran with him
in Montana night, led the attack,
took down a straggling deer.

Fed to fullness, retreated
with meat to den where pups ate,
nuzzled your nipples, curled

tight in soft fur. Sleep alone,
Luna, growl low, stretch long,
eyes closed from gold. Dream

a lover waits, scent heavy
in black wind. Heed his call,
hunt again by moonlight, feast.

Make the crimson last.
May you lie together till dawn,
panting in tall grass.

    (published by **Cascadia Rising Review**)

Bakery

You in front, I enter, excited,
am drawn first to the cream puffs,
gold, swollen, white filling
spilling out slender slits. I see
pies steaming off to the side,

want to dive in, especially the cherry.
Huge muffins, then cupcakes lure me,
protuberant domes of pink frosting
obviously eager to be licked.
Warm cinnamon rolls beckon too,

outer spirals tracing their way
to moist centers. I think I hear sirens
beyond the truffles. You seem rapt,
obviously tempted by hot éclairs,
the softest, bulging with cream,

icing dribbled along the top.
By then I am with the brioche,
light, sweet, round, wee,
begging me to use two fingers,
pry apart each delicate crust.

You revive, stretch, sway
your way to baguettes, hover,
choose the thickest, turn to go.
I come behind, a bit sad
our task here was to get bread.

(published by **Clover, A Literary Rag**)

The deadhover

"There is a little dead child in the pond —
one that has dreamed itself to death."
— Hans Christian Andersen,
"The daisy"

I begin to small against my lost life,
believe it time to fish at sundown,

mingle with black moths
whirled white in graying light.

Trust rod, line, fly to provide
cutthroat stopped mid-gasp

in tall grass. Slide a bright blade
along red bellies as growing dusk

covers bad memories stuck
in pooled blood. Wash the dead

in deep river, fling entrails, hearts
into night. Try to forget why

the hopeless call this place
a burial ground for shadows.

(published by **Sleet;** nominated
for the **Pushcart Prize**)

Door

Squeezed hallway, slim slit,
waiting's end, the pass

before. Breach, unbreathe,
scorn the fall, refuse the born.

Ignore pleas, turn, crawl,
leave behind the screaming door.

(published by **Convergence**)

Erasing black

I live a midnight vigil, lie still
in rain whipped by Montana wind,

try to dream my father back,
deliver a proper farewell —

will wrap myself in his gaze
as he recalls how wild rabbits

nibbled near his feet at sundown.
The motion sensor made darkness

spring to light. They froze, hopped,
froze again. If I feign sleep, maybe

they will arrive in small leaps,
him trailing with a smile to release

the loss, transform my dream
into a gateway to the past —

boy, age two, dad, paralyzed
by polio, alone in some hospital.

I refuse to eat, sit by the window,
breathless, wait. He lurches

on crutches from the night,
brings back a steady light.

(published by **Tipton Poetry Journal**)

Erratic tears

Off Oregon, Washington shores,
hulking above cove, beach, forest,
glacial erratics cry in silence.

They don't take a stance on much
at all, remain coolly apart
from debates of wind, clean water,

global warming, coal. Erratics
don't give a damn they are called
anomalous plodders, enigmas,

sporadic ho-hums. Seas sinking
Florida Keys, arbors kiwied
on Seattle streets mean nothing

to orphans ripped from Montana
to coast, abandoned for millennia now,
weeping, waiting for a bit of hope.

(published by **Whatcom Watch**)

Etiquette lesson
(with a nod to **White House Cookbook**, 1887)

Propriety while dining characterizes a man. Even
if obese, he must not scoot his chair too close
to the table. Also, he must never lean with belly
or elbows onto the table. He should not touch

any plate and should open his napkin and place it
across his right knee. In so doing, definitely
he should never grasp thigh or buttock of a lady
seated nearby. A gentleman holds fork and knife

properly, and in conversing, should not interrupt
anyone speaking to boast loudly of exploits
with the fairer sex. Especially, he does not speak
in a lustful way about his own daughter. He must

restrain a monstrous ego and give the semblance
of polite listening. He must also avoid vulgarities
during the meal even if he tends toward them
in his normal conduct of presidential business

when not dining. A gentleman eats and drinks
without making any sound and always keeps
his mouth shut while chewing food, as smacking
and slurping evoke disgust from other diners.

Etiquette means that he never uses his knife
to obtain butter; however, he may pick up
corn with one hand and eat it; he may also
pick up a bone and eat, but only with one hand.

Certainly if he feels a habitual urge, he must
definitely not use the free hand to grab a breast
of any lady nearby. A gentleman never drinks
from a cup with a spoon in it, and he should

never totally empty a container. In conversing,
he must not show hatred for those of darker
skin color or different language, because one
of them may be serving and certainly can hear

and think. A gentleman never breaks bread and
puts it into stew or soup, and if tempted because
of a slobby nature, must not eat off his knife
nor invert a spoon in his mouth even if it is

large enough easily to do so. Also, he must not
cool a drink or dish by blowing on it. In so
doing, he reveals himself to be uncultivated
and crude. Nor should he ever use his knife

to cut pastry, but only break and eat it with
a fork. At the end of a meal, a gentleman
does not cross his fork and knife; instead, he
places them side by side across the middle

of his plate. When rising from the table, he
never pushes his chair in, and should not
leave the room pompously while gazing
adoringly at himself in any nearby mirror.

(earlier version published by **Otoliths**)

Final blizzard

Last dream, sweep past
passed away, faith in winter storms

erased. Lost, chance to redact change,
bring tundra, forests back again.

Gone, too, deep rivers, streams,
springs, rainstorms bathing scree,

terminal moraine. Build a cairn,
rocks commodious to wee, jagged

to sky, martyred stone frozen white —
iced sign for final blizzard. Snow,

bury the saved, pile high.
Wake to glaciers marking graves.

(published by **Whatcom Watch**)

Fitting end

This being America, everyone's been offed,
mostly shot. We grabbed Colts, Berettas,
Glocks — fitting end for friendship, love,

forgiveness, trust. We blew away rapists,
burglars, thugs. Those of different skin
or faith, friends we hate, our boss.

Knocked off liars, waiters who whine,
text a lot, shoppers ramming carts,
stopping mid-aisle to tweet, flipping

us off. Cheating lovers, drivers
who stink-eye, speed, pass. We blasted
telemarketers last. Every trial,

over in a flash. Defendants,
lawyers, each one snuffed. Even judges
wasted jurors waving loaded guns.

    (published by **Mad Swirl**; republished
     by **Tipton Poetry Journal**)

Flat-line

Go, pack, leave. Be past tense,
deceased. Party, travel — jungle,
ruins, desert, dirty beach.

Museums, monuments, ghettos
back East. Fly home, collapse,
die alone in the street.

Family circle, land, search attic,
find gold, freezer, cash. Argue,
cry, fake grief — call attorney

likely to look up *brewhaha*,
find *brouhaha*, bill it as research,
discover a new will, bill that too.

>(published by **Mad Swirl**; republished
>in *The Best of Mad Swirl: 2018*)

God walks out of math proficiency exam

No need, really, calculus, physics,
trigonometry. She had every right
to leave — flat stones counted

skipped on ponds, graceful bend
of willows to the ground. Clouds fluffed
in morning sun, canyon shouts

echoed back at dusk.
Sin tallied on bark of trees,
feminine formula for infinity.

    (published by **Red River Review**)

I miss her more

I swear I do, now I know
it's become a competition.
I drive lonelier highways,

am more forlorn, weave farther
across the centerline. I also weep
wetter tears — not from pollen

or smoke stinging my eyes.
I suffer alone in quieter silence,
have no hope to transcend

the loss — just ask my boss.
I feel loss of love three times
as much, have notarized papers

to say my broken heart
breaks afresh five times a day.
I miss her so much, I beg you,

help me forget — drinks,
later tonight, my place,
a good way to begin.

    (published by **Kumquat Poetry Challenge**)

Inferno

Les Baux, rocky outcrop,
skyline castle, Celtic stronghold

above Provençal mining nightmare,
jagged inspiration for Dante.

Bleak peaks defying gravity.
Nine layers of tailings,

weeds scattered amid stone.
Nine lives of hell too

centuries before suspicion
free markets may not be

much good at all for those
who don't own goods,

aren't free — divine howl,
a blackened tragedy.

    (published by **Otoliths**)

Intertwined whisks

Whirl the egg, twirl in broth —
roux mustn't clot. Passion stirred,
hungry lives mixed up. Friend

of a friend, some texts, a date,
a waltz, a kiss, now this.
Like dancing or French cooking,

how to blend — or blending wrong.
Two whisks, intertwined,
different sauce, the same pot.

    (published by **Howl**)

Leaving at the break

It's a bad play, the set, a wreck,
Macbeth, a moron, lines, shrill,
frayed. Witches, no moxie, fretless

on a black stage, Macduff,
like you, lost since Lady left.
No way to be saved, one chance,

escape, act three, scene six.
Sneak by foyer grime, glitz,
warm wine tasting like crap.

Whisper farewell to Banquo, fall
into night, love, a leg fractured,
jagged bone sticking out.

    (published by **Tipton Poetry Journal**)

Like a fenced-in dog

I'll wear paths behind barbed wire, deep,
start a tunnel every three feet. Pit bull,

wait my chance — growl, howl, foam,
bite any hand holding a phone. I know

moist treats, meaty bones will be
distant memory once I escape,

hit the street. I'll crap lawns, kill cats,
chase Amazon trucks, police, priests,

make veterinarians not charge a fee —
torture hydrants with angry pee.

    (published by **Mad Swirl**)

Low-tide triage

Winter again, beach fire lit, ocean mist,
moonlight raking stranded starfish in,
nature's hint — save something,

salvage spring. Kneel on cold sand,
iced, damp, assess the earth, the sick.
Breathe deep, trim ragged edges

of igneous heart, slice off conscience,
at least the darkened bits. Somehow,
avoid amputation of the ending.

    (published by **Sleet Magazine**)

Making cadaver scents

Smells of death — stirred, brewed,
grave way to train rescue dogs,

saviors of the strayed, forsaken,
betrayed, lost. Dead, vanished

into bottles — avalanche, revenge,
fire, flood. Scents so strong

salvation turns out moot,
reclaimed life after breathlessness

another lie too. Those remaining,
missions aside, finally find sleep.

They dream the cuckolds are alive,
buried in snow, deeper than deep.

   (published by **Otoliths**)

The math

adds up, given the time spent
figuring ways to stay alive.
Join health club, subtract weight,
do yoga, every new kind

of exercise. Limit junk food,
get sleep, plus shots for measles,
tetanus, flu. Life kept like a lover
on the sly — think no one knows,

divide the family, deny she, too,
someday will go. You, remainder
alone to crunch numbers, buy time,
escape avalanche, tornado,

flood, crashed car or plane.
Calculate ways to flee a fire,
not drown in stream, ocean, river,
lake. Multiply odds to survive

a quake — pitch tent out back,
hoard water, meds, food, supplies.
Believe we've solved the sky,
count black stars as they arrive.

    (published by **Convergence**)

Miasma

With riot dogs, let them sniff
one hand — makes it safe to pet.
For police, a grin, stay back

ten feet, arms out, palms up.
If clubbed, cover head, close eyes,
cringe, pretend to sleep.

Dream away leaders, dense,
intent — willing to torch villages
just to catch the scent.

    (published in ***Whatcom Writes Anthology***)

Natural orders

The first decrees — lip-gloss fresh air
we breathe, pixie-cut all trees,

dab perfume on winding streams.
Brush a blush on glaciers, floes,

Arctic ice, perm stars lighting up night.
Blow-dry canyons, valleys,

mountain, crags. Mousse mesas,
prairies, all that's flat. Eye-line crows,

buffalo, deer, their fawns. Wax
the ozone layer until it's gone.

Thick mascara blots the sun, makes
living in darkness beautiful for us.

   (published by **Whatcom Watch**)

Nibblers

I dream garra rufa fish
feed toothless on my bare feet,

nibble dead skin from toes,
heels, my soles, my soul.

Evil ones, piranha of sorts,
leap clear of water, aim

for my chest — like you, rip me
open, devour arteries, ventricles,

everything vein. I am left to pray
for holy stents again.

    (published by **Howl**)

No leaving

Mostly I keep death out of mind,
pretend path to the end to be
a natural flow, sometimes wend.
Then webcam streams online

B.C. eagle nest in alder tree —
below, a factory. At first, pure joy
on screen, parents, watchful,
sleek, nest ringed by twigs,

two fuzzed eaglets, lurching,
eager to eat. Eight hundred viewers
watch dad bring a dead squirrel in,
flesh soon ripped to bite-sized strips.

Mom returns, he flaps away, she, now
feathered shelter against the rain.
Next meal, flopping sockeye, still alive,
eaglets gobble belly, then insides.

I turn away before the end.
Overnight, one baby dies, by dawn
dried-blood-stuck to mom's soft side.
We view a frantic dance — scrape

lifeless body over the edge. Workers
arrive, unaware one baby remains,
not the pair. I mourn all day.
She won't leave. Her gold eyes stare.

(published by **Windfall**)

No more argument

He surges at me, spews
an armada of reasons

to reject climate change,
forget carbon, love cars,
trucks, planes. Lays praise

on factories, damns Earth First,
the jerks, mere pessimists,

eager to hate. A loud knock,
the door, then two. I open it
a crack, have time to say,

the Pacific's here to see you.

> (published by **Sleet Magazine**;
> republished by **Whatcom Watch**)

Not stomping I LOVE YOU in the snow

A fire dance would be more in line —
cremate fields gone winter white,

kick frozen sparks at gray-black sky.
Something angry, fierce. Slice my heart,

see stomping cannot hold. Know *YOU*
would never melt, useless to try.

I should have seen love moves on,
not waste time, freeze feet,

in mid-pas de deux let words I write
lie breathless, flat, deceased, iced —

though in a row, left to right.
Remember she always hated snow,

believed romance the best fiction,
was quick to pack and go.

    (published by **San Pedro River Review**)

One thousand seconds

No motion permitted, lie back, hope
dermatologist, Lance, knows enough —

laser in hand, can scorch evil layer
off cheek in sixteen minutes plus.

Eyes closed to each flash, time to dream
womb, baby, dark to light. More sparks,

face teened, back seat, homecoming queen
staring up from underneath. No luck — wake,

only one hundred seconds gone, age
not wiped away, nine hundred left to face.

(published by **Red River Review**)

Panic knot

False belief — only the chosen
don't feel weak, won't scream,

stifle urge to flee, excrete.
Woven ball of fear inside,

no good to cry, fret, lose sleep.
Gallows ritual, also useless guide —

adjust hood, pull noose tight,
step aside, wave goodbye. Go

in style — close eyes, yawn a curse,
fall asleep before the jerk.

    (published by **Otoliths**)

Poplars

Arctic wind, autumn-coaxed,
tell ghost trees, release red leaves

chilled gold, let them float.
Northern lights on polar nights

try to pulse stark groves to life.
Nowhere to go, iced by snow,

the poplars creak, sway,
dream of spring, dance in place.

    (published by **Whatcom Watch**)

Reading

Famous writers seem especially adept —
drift in at the last moment,

blue jeans, wrinkled shirt, tweed jacket,
hair messed. At the podium,

they smile, wink at young women,
offer excuses for being late —

*stopped to watch a clock tower burn,
heard it chime out in fright,*

saw blackened doves take flight.
They reach into ragged pack

or wrinkled bag, finally bring out
a new volume of their work.

The moment may be near —
first, search pockets for glasses,

ask for water, room temp, no ice.
Adjust microphone, tap it, say

the book is for sale afterward —
at last, begin reading. They mouth

each word as if it were the nub
of a savory fried-chicken bone.

We clap eagerly, urging them
to suck out every last bit of marrow.

(published by **The Bond Street Review**)

Resigning from being messiah

Not all it was cracked up
to be. Plus,

I had other plans.
More than you can imagine.

An array, bevy, plethora,
in fact, a piranha.

    (published by **Hobart**)

Roseate

Dancers queued, poem to begin,
surfers intense, thousand-yard stare,

climber below summit, ready
for thin air. Mountain unconquered,

wave out of reach, lyric not written,
footwork seized — tango, sonnet,

ocean, peak. All paused, in step,
ready to keep time — calm,

waiting for dawn, breathtaking view,
the coming moment, pas de deux.

    (published by **Otoliths**)

Several supple weasels

weave like your memory, sleek
through trees, find slippery ways

to avoid the rain, slink away
deep into murky streams.

Leave me dazed, confused,
ready to believe amygdalae,

the almond-shaped mass
in each cerebral hemisphere,

gray matter steeping the brain.
Make me embrace emotion,

whether or not I want,
like anger, hate, this sly pain.

    (published by **Convergence**)

Vast silence
(with a nod to Ted Chiang)

A people conquered, stripped
of land, children, homes. Captives
for life. Language forbidden —

pleas for food, blanket, drink
permitted only by sign, wave,
blink. With the last elder's death,

vanished, stories, songs, poems.
Gone, every dance, painting, play.
At the end, only vast silence.

On cell wall, a farewell, scratched
in English, the lettering, crude —
you be good we forgive you

    (published by **Clover, A Literary Rag**)

When I went out to hang myself
(with a nod to Alex Vouri)

I found laundry filled the line. Removed
black panties doing a frantic dance,

pirate flags spanking sky above a rigid plank.
Made enough space for head, throat,

pinned them to a flimsy, graying rope.
I was driven to hold sway over baskets

of rank adjectives and damp complaints
against a miasmatic world. Began

my final descent — a naive onlooker noted
the world smells as fresh as fabric softener.

   (published by **Red River Review**)

Poems 2017

Almost

I promise we'll hold hands
dawn to dusk, dream one dream,
sleep intertwined. Cuddle

each night, spot the same star,
wish the same wish. I'll give
endless gifts, kiss the deepest kiss.

We'll eat the same food, split
every dish. Share one job,
co-sign loans, carpool to work,

embrace all the way home.
A perfect love — or very close.
Pretty much one dream,

nearly the same wish. A few gifts,
quite a deep kiss. More or less,
every dish. At least one loan.

Part of the way home. Romance
full of bliss — almost. At least,
in the beginning, quite a bit.

    (earlier version published by **Foliate Oak**)

Beginning of forgetting
(with a nod to Marguerite Duras)

I was lost before I was lost,
couldn't find myself in Bannack,
Dillon, Polaris, Grant.

Missed me in Missoula, Dixon,
even my mirror looking back.
Seems I can't get a compass right,

leave Montana behind, in peace,
reach the Snake, the Columbia,
Camas, Astoria, the sea.

A lover who loves rescue said
go, find deserted beach,
plant strands of wire, wait

for spring, see if barbs grow.
Better, I take a place near Blaine,
maybe Birch Bay, sleep alone,

dream myself a philosopher
of loss. Like Duras, map
a way out. Find losing, itself,

not to be the finale —
but a great darkness falling,
the beginning of forgetting.

A way to kindle hope —
to become certain the end
does not become the end.

(earlier version published by **Cirque**)

Benchmark

Gone, without wings she flies,
no backward glance, no time
for the massacred behind,

disemboweled — stark ending
witnessed by a murder of crows
who caw loudly before they go.

Hope could be the benchmark —
those with too little, soaring north
in dark night — with too much,

south, searching for rotted sky.
All not finding god becoming —
nor becoming god — proclaim

who dies, permit just anyone
to scavenge black coffins,
no entrails left inside.

  (published by **Convergence**)

Books on the way out
(with a nod to Glen Larum)

"My life is all I've got."
—Richard Hugo
in ***The Triggering Town***

Sun on horizon, you read an ending
like Milton's — gone to blindness,
looking for light. It's time to flee,

drive highways west — feedlots,
cattle queued, barns, hay
freshly mown, slaughterhouse below.

Finally one runway, control tower
rising like a phoenix from fields,
promising hope, rest not far away.

You wend to town, cruise Main,
pass bars, one lonely church,
ancient stores late in rot.

A pickup rolls by, gun rack full,
pit-bull growling in back, seat-belt
painted on the driver's shirt

to fool john law. Hotel flies
a huge flag. You stay quiet, wish
your belt would hide the iPad

tucked in your pants, deep.
Too tired to sleep, wi-fi coming
next year, you walk the street,

search for books — Hemingway,
Paradise Regained, Silko, Alexie,
Lycidas, anything in ink.

Night brings black, town cafe,
muddy coffee, charred steak,
burnt toast — wheat, not white.

The grizzled cook serves a smile,
says bookstore's at the airport,
past security, on the right.

    (published by **Tipton Poetry Journal**)

Cairn

Cascades meadow, peak above
pointing through mist. I gather
rocks, some annular, others flat.

You set each atop another,
gingerly construct a column
ascending from a mossy base.

Stones of different size give it
a ragged look. Sometimes,
shale supports basalt as large

as your heart or breasts. I recline
beside my pile of rocks, study you
from behind, hold my breath.

You bend, lithe, carefully adjust
the placement — stand, pause,
assess pillar's stability, its rise

to a brightening sky. I hope
it takes you all summer
to finish this cairn.

>(published by **Windfall**;
>republished by **River Poets Journal**)

Cairnly power

No lame balloon man goat-footed
to inspire, no

widening gyre
no falcon, windhover,

wimpling wing whistling wee,
alluring, random gaps

put in, sweet sweat,
stamina not smalling in the distance,

she hopes I rise, cairnly power
coming from a small tablet.

    (published by **Harbinger Asylum**)

Call waiting

My phone takes selfies, snaps pics,
has maps if I go on trips — Blaine, Sequim,
Wellpinit, Twisp. Lets me play old games —

Angry Birds, Super Mario jumping
from place to place. Newer ones, too —
Pokémon Go, Clash of Clans, Dead Space.

Orders pizza, counts calories, pulse rate,
my few steps. Checks Facebook, weather,
tells when the sun rises or sets.

Shows YouTube clips, movies, hip-hop,
Taylor Swift. I can Instagram, Tweet,
hike online with virtual friends,

ask Siri where truth begins, ends.
Also makes calls — haven't tried it yet.
I did text Dad to pass the salt.

    (published by **Poetry Quarterly**)

Centered
(with a nod to Stephen Crane)

The universe said to a man,
Sir, I exist all around you.

Great, the man replied, *great,
but are you gluten-free?*

    (published by **Whatcom Watch**)

Damp dance

Mountain hike, summer thoughts
join memory — you, me, years ago,
alone, first date, sudden storm.

Sheltered by boughs, we shiver, listen
to rain, for warmth, intertwine.
Each splash becomes a damp dance,

wet pirouette amid tall grass.
Hot breath on cheek, neck,
passing lips, at last, a half-kiss.

One more, deep, full, intense —
bright sun, lull in the squall
bring an end to the beginning

of it all. You glide past puddles
on our path home. I fill each track
in my desire to stay close.

    (published by **Otoliths**)

Executive orders

Pathetic, sad, blacktop the trees,
they bloom disease. Brick in

air we breathe. Drill moonlight
as it arrives, also glaciers, floes,

Arctic ice. Back-fill mesas, plains,
everything flat. Strip-mine rivers,

streams, frack green plants.
Spray buffalo, crows, antelope,

clearcut bees, butterflies, goats.
Driftnet muskrats, bats, deer,

their fawns, pave the whales
until they're gone. Build a wall,

blot out the sun. Life in darkness
will be cool for us.

    (published by **Howl**)

Existential diagram
(with a nod to Anna Eblen and Rick Popish)

I dream I am a verb midway
on some penciled line stretching
to the horizon in both directions.

A dark upright separates me
from the lithe subject, who finds
a way to seduce me. Again,

I become linked to a lover,
am still unable to talk fractals
before her first cup of coffee.

She has no hope for a complex life,
say, lying with an alluring gerund
or principled participle in control

of her entire sentence. Certainly,
not going wild, locked at the hips
with an infinitive in hot blackness.

(published by **Harbinger Asylum**)

Existential haircut

Not funeral home nor church,
white sheet draped over me,

mirrors repeat endless backs
of my head into far distance.

Each grows more wee
till the faint version of myself

does not seem to exist.
A tiny barber dances razor

to sharpness on leather strap,
finishes me off,

dutifully scraping away
even my smallest reflection.

>   (published by **Dual Coast Magazine**;
>   accepted by **Windsor Review**)

First sign of wind

I am alone again, breathless, covered
by blankets of white. A full moon
cuts birch branches lifeless

in Coeur d'Alene night. The rays slice
my heart. Ice hangs from the gutter,
waits for spring. I only see

the hanging. With luck, I will dream
primroses poke through snow at dawn,
bloom at the first sign of wind.

    (published by **Third Wednesday**)

Full of yourself

Mirrors line dining room,
one smile reflected, you,

again and again. In soup, too,
face shimmered back,

you looking trim — no lovers
added, no friends to toss in.

Full of yourself,
a seven-course binge.

    (published by **Red River Review**)

Gone to rubble
(with a nod to Nejat Hulusi)

Husband thirty years, he writhes,
shakes in bed, calls for another soda,
this time after she leaves the room.

He has peed himself again, third time
since dawn, urine returning butt to red.
She changes diaper, preps for doctor trip,

fears a repeat of last week — shower,
scrub, shampoo, rinse. He shits
as the toweling begins. Another rinse,

dried, dressed, he pees.
Wash, ointment, fresh diaper,
finally ready, walker to the Ford

promised to still be hers when savings
are gone. He asks to ride his bike,
wants a pop, drinks, pees the seat.

She screams, *why, why, why
can't you tell me you have to go.*
Parkinson's marriage, no way back.

Earthquake, gone to rubble,
trembling only the beginning,
all major destruction coming later.

(published by **Black Fox Literary Magazine**)

Homeless night watchman
(with a nod to Steve Giordano)

Job's for a week, start at dusk,
the pay, eight bucks — don't sleep.

Park van behind the station, be gone
at dawn. Dial 9-1-1 if thieves

steal gas from the pumps.
Say you're a guard, call my cell,

then take off. I'll give a wave
when I'm done with the cops.

Talk to the guy who opens —
he'll have chips, cheese,

Coke, some leftover meat.
Use the back door to leave.

Key opens restroom only —
no showering in the sink.

(published by **Windsor Review**)

Hope synchs

Uplifting, the anticipation, so weird
it droops, disappears — gone like drug
to vein, bloody sleeve rolled up

then down again. Chosen path,
moving flat, hopeless keep right,
bags closed, clutched tight.

Others pass, glide by fast,
intent on flight, the end,
rogue church, meek within.

Perfect time to writhe, pray, sweat
crème brûlée sin away, hoping
to be granted whatever.

    (published by **Otoliths**)

Inflicting scars

Much like us, minerals gouge others
softer than themselves. Topaz
will scratch quartz, which can gash

gold, itself, cowering heaped, no way
to scrape emeralds or jade.
The mineral color when smashed flat —

streak line or streak, say green
for malachite. Diamonds, like you,
though rarely crushed, have a streak

of white. Beautiful, the hardest,
at their will they cut a deep line
into everything, even rubies.

To see really red streaks, scars
down far, take a closer look
at the bottom half of my heart.

>   (published by **Convergence**)

Long stumps of hope

Forgiveness is natural, you say,
like change — it's half a heartbeat.
Blood, pumped out, flows in.

Waves, depleted, retreat
to sea. Wet tears later dry.
Broken hearts heal, pain subsides.

Suddenly I believe you,
after not — see how loss
can change to gain, buds in May

replace winter, snow, decay.
Lovers like you take back
the beloved who strayed.

War, too, goes, peace grows.
Children who cowered alone
put wounds out of mind,

smile at soldiers marching by.
They play without legs
on long stumps of hope.

(published in ***Whatcom Writes Anthology***)

Love you more

now I see it's a competition.
I laughed longer at your jokes

than you did, mine. I apologized
in half the time. Plus, I cried

wetter tears, sighed bigger sighs.
When you left, I felt deeper loss,

greater stress. I also miss you
more — or less.

    (published by **Gulf Coast Writers Association**)

Migratory text

Ritual journey, known trip
unknown. Tunnel behind,

vaginal, dim. Locked
in memory, blissful ride

amid anemone, cosmos,
buttercup, rose. Lover

now silent, breathing low,
thumbs busy on her phone.

    (published by **Mad Swirl**; republished
    in ***Best of Mad Swirl: 2017***)

Montana condolences, of a kind

Visit neighbor next farm over,
three silos, combines, a section

of wheat. His wife dying,
lung cancer, give her eight weeks.

I hang my head, shuffle,
see mud, clumped thick, both feet.

Only know to say, *yep, well,*
helluva winter, heard futures

might be headed up. Whiskey
at home if you need a drink.

(published by **Third Wednesday**)

Montana harvest
(with a nod to Margaret Atwood)

Garden ritual, early fall,
I try again to re-grow love.
Silent, we kneel, pull clumps

of crab grass, buttercup,
miss the roots. A few plants
have survived dry dirt,

spindly, anemic. Weeds
I raked into piles she burns
like witches, as if to scorch away

my evil. We sleep together, apart.
I listen to her breathe,
dream a grizzly rips up darkness —

manage to harvest radicchio,
chard, red cabbage, a few beets.
At dawn, the autumn sun bleeds.

(published by **Third Wednesday**)

No absolution

If you think you're beaten,
you are. Again. Even though

you took him back.
Believe he will change,

he won't. Your boat, oar,
his stroke. Lost love,

lost life, lost raft.
Deep ocean, last rites.

(published by **Otoliths**)

No day to be named after a uvula
(with a nod to Alex Vouri)

I dream I am a famous tenor
stripped of my tucked-in shirt.

I rehearse in the shower,
later bellow high notes

into an ice-cave, echoes there
adding strength to my refrain.

The opera fails in Australia.
My songs leak counter-clockwise

down a plastic drain, lose power
at the bend, leave me out of breath

before the aria ends. Nameless.
Another guilty white guy

who will only be remembered
if I put all my shit in a museum.

    (published by **Poetry Pacific**)

No more robbery

Mount Baker above, you collect rocks —
basalt, granite, shale — hand them
to me. I place one on another,
construct a cairn, each stone

jutting jagged. Some skipping rocks
support others the size of ptarmigans.
I need this column to be strong,
survive until the threatening storm

is impeached. A historian once noted
growth for the sake of growth
is the philosophy of the cancer cell.
Not always, not here. My pillar

joins others, a thousand of them
staggering into fierce wind, resisting
Earth's great robbery. Together,
the cairns hold up the sky.

   (earlier version published by **Whatcom Watch**)

No release

Dreams of her swim in again
like red-gilled trout lying deep

in a Montana stream. They school,
eager to feed — hold back,

skittish, fearful of being hooked,
flung into tall grass, lying still,

gasping only at the end.
One after another flash past

my Black Ghost skipping by —
each a gold, green streak

reminding me what I catch
I cannot release.

    (published by **Convergence**)

Not biting

I wade with pack, rod, flies
onto the freeway, slosh across
white stripes to the far side.

Fish for a time in the carpool lane.
No strikes. Cast deep into tunnels,
swirling eddies at exits.

Still nothing. Near dusk, I pitch
my tent on the median, fry a slab
of Spam, huddle by campfire

reflected red on a yield sign.
It could be I have reached
my limit, put her memory

out of mind. A fuchsia sun
flashes low, turns orange to gold,
glowing purple — then she goes.

I rise in total darkness,
break camp before rush-hour,
take the long way home.

>(published by **Clover, A Literary Rag**;
>republished in ***Speakeasy***)

Odd

now no cards to send,
write *happy holidays,*

lick glue, add stamps.
Busy instead, stand off,

emoji, blot out friends,
send a text, tweet

cruel joke, harass gay,
label woman slut or tramp,

let pass who groped whom,
grabbed whose ass. Easy, alone,

head down, virtuality, together,
busy thumbing phone. Sadder

in a way, loving love less
than loving to hate.

    (published by **Mad Swirl**)

Parenthetical

Walls curve gently up, high prisons,
like your hips. Poets inside can't glimpse

sentence end, never see final words
drive meaning home, satiated by dash,

terse period, giddy explanation point.
New Yorker favorites like Alexie

don't mount a rescue mission, scale
bowed barriers, belay down, let

bad sonnets go. Overshadowed,
the trapped quiver, sadness looming

parenthetical at both ends. Like me,
only iambic lovers dream them free.

   (published by **Harbinger Asylum**)

Please

be seated, this poem is about to begin.
No run-of-the-mill greeting card rhyme

with lots of pop and pow. More subtle,
nuance lodged in metaphors, meaning

ripped from jagged words, obscure,
like graffiti on a brick wall, scribbled

in black ink, at night. Imagine
an outlaw poet on the run, wounded,

firing blank verse at a posse in pursuit,
missing, putting out the sun.

(published by **Otoliths**)

Question of humility
(with a nod to Richard Hugo)

Dream some festival to honor
a great writer. Dozens of poets

lounge by mineral springs
hidden under trees. Hot water

mixes with cold, ringed stones
create pools different in heat.

All drink bourbon, wine, brandy,
the good stuff — it's free.

They circle a fire, grow silent
in fading light. The great one

rises from steam, asks poets
at his feet — *if I were to place*

three poems high in night sky,
what question would you speak:

Which poems are placed there?
Or, is mine among the three?

    (published by **Fragments**)

Ravel

Begin to knit a new design,
decide if and when to forgive.

Do you keep her memory inside
for what to breathe for next

or toss, like moth, to candle flame,
gossamer flash gone gray

to ash — raveled smoke on the rise,
searching for an end to night?

    (published by **Spindrift**)

Read-out

Your lover lies still, white.
Listen to her breathe. Stare

at the read-out, red numbers
swimming by. Follow the I.V. flow down,

pause at a bend where the tube
darts beneath starched sheets.

Dream back half a life — campfire,
tent, creek. Cast out thin line

on the blank screen. Hope you fish
together, downstream.

    (published by **Spindrift**)

Sea change

Floe broken off, mere speck now,
bear cubs whine, drift south.
They prowl the ice.
Mom dives in, swims to them —
for quite some time.

(published by **Whatcom Watch**)

Still glow
(with a nod to Albert Camus)

Heads down, no way to say *sorry,*
mistake, we drag laden canoe
to the beach, paddle choppy water,
her behind, steering.

We churn up a narrow channel,
hope current won't take hold,
sweep everything downstream.
Camp pitched without speaking,

soup heated over anemic fire,
we swallow hot broth of remorse.
Forgiveness hangs in smoke
below sun turning cutthroat red.

We place sleeping bags far apart,
try not to shiver, lie alone,
sob as meteors trail to black.
I dream I am not lost,

the sun casts no shadows,
and somehow I escape night.
Coals still glow at dawn.
The canoe and she aren't gone.

>   (published by **Harbinger Asylum;**
>   different version, "Still glow at dawn,"
>   published in 2017 by **Howl**)

Storm

Her lacy bra lies on the bed,
white cups open upward
as if ready to catch every drop
from a coming storm. I tiptoe
to the window. Clouds loom,
huge. It smells like rain.

    (published by **Clover, A Literary Rag**)

Summer hymn

Metro stop. July. Sun, hot,
high — a voice behind —

rest-home lawn, some old guy,
wheel-chaired, waves at me.

I wander over, give him five.
Holiday's complete, he says,

*now you've come home.
Mom's shopping, back soon*

with pies, tree, presents, lights.
My bus arrives, I search my pack,

find a gift — turkey sandwich,
wrapped in white, no ribbon,

no bow. He smiles. I lean close,
hum a few bars of Silent Night.

    (published by **Red River Review**)

Sweet peace

Pinned down many days, we sent
for a beekeeper to rid us

of the machine gun nest.
She arrived, dressed in fine mesh,

gloves, khaki coveralls so thick
the enemy must have believed

she was a platoon, company,
maybe an entire brigade.

Wand of dark smoke, brush,
like a feather duster swept

gunner, ammo, nest, the entire war
into a cardboard box. We gasped

when she marched to a distant hive
as if carrying only a single swarm.

(published by **Harbinger Asylum**)

Viral in Norway
(with a nod to Alex Vouri)

City street, fine brasserie, slip inside,
find a seat. Shake piled snow

off cuckold. Sip Pernod,
study the menu, name its font.

Not Arial, Gil sans. Feast on lamb,
frog legs, foie gras, Pastis gascon.

Top it off — coffee, St. Rémy,
crème brûlée. Close your eyes,

dream a new lover arrives.
You move to Provence, become

a chef. Tweet recipes. In bed.
In French. The Mistral blows sheets

of phyllo dough down the street.
Your dream life goes viral in Norway.

(published by **Sleet Magazine**)

Wedding rescue

Reflection, men's room mirror,
outdoor wedding, clear sky,
groom, pierced, tattooed,

struggling, panic in eyes.
Black tux, on right, nice fit,
he wrestles loose tie —

like marriage gone bad,
stretched thin, unknotted again.
Stranger turned savior,

I offer to drape my neck.
Wide end, short, hang to right,
snake over tip. Squeeze,

use two fingers, spread slit.
Slip it in, pull down, adjust
a bit. Loosen the noose,

drop over groom's head.
Nose ring bright, he smiles.
I pull the knot tight.

    (earlier version published
      by **Tipton Poetry Journal**)

Who's counting

Number's up, six feet round, clock
turned empty, work week, love,
ticked down. Time to plant wire,

strands coiled dark in soil,
taking root, rusted gold,
sharpened barbs about to grow.

Garden fenced with kale,
four joined rows bristling out
weasels, rats, even cats —

black ones, tails eleven inches,
white ones, female, sleek,
claws measure twelve.

(published by **Otoliths**)

Working with wind at Canyon de Chelly
(with a nod to D'von Charley)

Flute to lips near precipice rim,
Navajo man bends a bit,

catches breeze, sends haunting song
down to ruins, stream, jimsonweed,

salt cedar, Russian olive trees.
Echoes dance off sandstone cliffs,

drift past women herding goats.
Ducks etched green, gold, red

on canyon walls, wait to swim
should Chinle Wash flow wide again.

Tourists buy photos, CDs. Navajo youth
play small flutes under piñon trees.

    (published by **Howl**)

Poems 2016

Afghanistan misery index

After piling dead babies
high enough
to reach the flashing traffic light,
we climb slowly up,
being careful not to fall,
then turn
the suffering bastard
off.

(published by **Red River Review**)

After the falls

comes, of course, winter —
not that demise leads inevitably so,

nor seasons wending circular paths
one to the other, spring

to summer, but winter in the sense
that falls mean sudden departures

from state of privilege, deceptions,
unseen cliffs, sudden stairs,

financial setbacks so severe
your Porsche is gone,

along with the women you primed
with wine and fast talk,

you remember, the Radisson bar
near Niagara, where you promised

a happy life forever, together,
after the honeymoon, after the falls.

(published by **Prole Press**)

Always speaking truth to power

even when the powerful
are only serving coffee

labels you as outcast,
geek, unbearable know-it-all.

Just an asshole, really. Mimes,
watchful, still, seemingly meek,

shun the pricks unless they grind
dark roast into the street.

    (published by **The Curious Record**)

The bitter end

When she becomes remote,
draws black curtains over green eyes,
keeps you, your touch, at bay,

know no way exists
to foster hope. You see, she's folded
your memory — creased it really,

really creased it — placed it
at the end of the scrapbook she calls
her life. All bits tossed away for good —

for you, for bad. She's whirled off
in dirty wind, gone coffin gray.
Time for you to fade, decay.

    (published by **Convergence**)

**Card from Montana, only snow
on the cover**
(with a nod to Lola Reidelbach)

Well, I'm getting older, another year gone.
Weather only knows how to blizzard,

nothing goes on. Can't get out much.
Town has casinos now, play them

sometimes, don't win though —
they are rigged. Kids still live around.

Oldest cleans at the rest home,
youngest just retired, so nothing.

Middle one drives snow plow,
got a foster kid, he's on crack.

I dread winter, my cousin died —
it was a stroke. That's about all.

Hope this finds you happy and well,
with the snow all gone by fall.

> (published by **Trestle Creek Review**;
> different version, "Card from Idaho, only snow
> on the cover," published in 2016 by **Cirque**)

Claiming, not owning

Forest trail vanished in pine,
we hike, neither one following,

find spongy moss winds
by a faint spring coaxed up

to half-light. Its water tests
boundaries, breaks free, forms

small pools below. They fill,
spill into others — each finger

escaping any intention to hold.
The tiny rivulets trickle alone

until a second sliver, a third,
then one more, join. Together,

they stream private paths down,
each resisting being owned.

We choose separate ways
across their defiant flows.

    (published by **Otoliths**)

Diagramming love

I dream myself next to you
on a thin, penciled line.

I am a predicate — the action —
separated from you, subject

of my love. I hope to awaken,
find I am really a linking verb

and this sentence,
not in passive voice.

    (published by **Bellingham Herald**)

Dreaming on key

Learn young to hoard, suck in air,
don't breathe — lock, no release,
midnight dreams conjured

on cue, sleepless master of control.
Not simple, like Kegel, ten-second hold,
gone from gold, in reverse, now clear,

pee upstream, never mind Jung,
Ganges, any leper's scream.
Truth be told, hope's gone bad,

turned fantasy — fake belief we foresee,
dream on key, spot death, the cheat,
card hidden up her lacy sleeve.

    (published by **Tipton Poetry Journal**)

Drying tear, sullen sky

In your own desert, paint
a lone birch, no other green
being seen. Brush dipped

in white, stroke extra wide
for trunk, main branches up —
use mint for leaves, ash-gray,

bark sheets, life peeling away.
If no ladder to reach top,
paint a tall one of those.

Colors, water all packed,
climb, paint the high limbs.
Reach far out, daub sun,

sky too. Dream of rain,
swirl in a gathering storm.
Make each drop oblong

like a tear drying in sullen sky.
Use a slim brush, tip so fine
your still-life stands out.

>(published by **Otoliths**;
>accepted by **Spindrift**)

Fake dreams

In them, you are fit, witty,
great in bed, have some friends.

Lottery winner, no job to hate,
you wear designer clothes,

collect fine art, give trips to sibs.
You buy beggars burgers,

chocolate, gin — gun down raiders
breaking in your place, suck back

angry words, out-pun cuckolds
lurking around your mate.

You bask in children's praise,
bring mom alive again,

have clear streams to fish.
Your heart beats on its own.

You get back to sleep
when you wish.

    (published in ***Mapping water***)

Family of widows

All things relative, the earth turns,
permits off-sprung rays to spangle,
children of the ocean to retreat.

By comparison, nouns, concrete,
verbs, taut with action, lie squirming,
babies of the pen. A few will live,

stories deserving of an ending.
Not about happiness, salvation,
even so much about love.

More, narrative of stars, moon —
light heaviness, a family of widows
asleep, weighted down by the sun.

>   (published by **Cirque**)

Final say

Religious youth sneaks Glock
to school, prevents murder spree,

kills weird dude before he shoots.
Students flee, hands over heads —

boy with Glock accidentally shot,
blown away by a Swat-team cop.

Father come to save his only son
snuffs sniper with a backup gun.

Passing priest takes revenge,
pulls out Uzi, blasts the dad —

gets popped too, shot from above
out of love, the final say.

    (published by **Convergence**)

Finally talking to a guru in India

In the beginning, phone-tree,
long branch, press one for savior.

Time on hold to ponder,
do we cease to exist or exist

to cease. Me, out of it, off
a bit, high on tea, so much so

need to call for help, not visit
spiritualist, where folks queue,

air kiss, woo-woo session
with lost wives, lovers, of whom

I have not any left. Guru hisses,
low-pitched, *complete the reversal,*

fetch redemption, undo each wrong.
Be less bad than old me, better

than the new. Silence does not mean
no answer. He hangs up on me too.

    (published by **Mad Swirl**)

Half lithe

Season of absolution in full sway,
late spring, coarse snow gone

from white to gray. Most piles
shallow, a few still deep.

You, on occasion, able to smile,
get good sleep, play outside,

make angels in vacant drifts.
Sometimes, remember to forget,

forgive. Her memories brushed aside,
heaviness melting, soon half lithe.

   (published by **Prole Press**)

Homage

Steep climb to peak along icy creek,
I round a bend, glimpse through trees

line of women, ridge overhead,
sweaters, jeans, panties off.

They face the summit, arms spread,
heads back, eyes closed, breasts taut,

pointed upslope. *In wan sun,*
bitter wind, we sisters bare ourselves,

pay homage to you, Mother Earth.
Give us inspiration, hope.

Face red, eyes kept low,
I creep downstream, fully clothed.

    (published by **Carnival**)

If God searches your room

it goes without saying
she will find Legos and games

stuffed into closet, dirty socks
tucked under bed, candy wrappers

shoved far back in the second drawer.
What cannot be discussed

is how faith was lost,
hidden away so deep,

out of the blue comes this lack
of trust, sudden need to sift

your stuff. Better not bring up
betrayal, question why she

freaks out, intrudes. Head down,
keep busy with the broom.

    (published by **Mad Swirl**)

Light found to have weight

Fly rod in hand, sun nearly set,
I've seen how burdened brightness
affects the cast, slows line
looping through red sky

to tease some riffle on the dark,
far side. Heavy light brings on
a ribboned splash, scatters rainbows
before my Black Ghost drifts in.

At dawn, light rises, groggy,
barely able to clear meadow grass,
staggers from carrying all that dew
layered on by summer night.

Later, laden by midday heat,
it quits skim of lake, gives in,
lies deep with bass,
shifting shadow under lily pads.

Weighed down, too, like light,
the dying cease to resist,
succumb, sink to blackness,
having finally reached their limit.

(published by **Carcinogenic Poetry**)

Limerick 1

Subdued city people were keen
to copy St. Pat's party scene —
a wild bingo night
brought yawns by first light,
giddy giving way to serene

    (published by **Bellingham Herald**)

Limerick 2

Food a pale lime, beer half-green too,
laid-back city bash misconstrued
as wild Irish gig
with drink, song and jig —
innocence unjustly subdued

    (published by **Bellingham Herald**)

Lit exam

A sonnet is to salvation
as Milton, to squid, confess,

bind, climbing a steep ridge.
Sestina, to redemption

as Keats to grieve, resign,
whale, falling off cliffs.

Villanelle, to remembrance
as Bishop, to church, prayer,

veil, gutting fresh fish. Canto,
to hatred as Rich, to loss,

failure, God, filleting black cod.
Epitaph, to hope as Alexie,

to smudge, forgiveness, sole,
burning a white cross.

>   (published by **Switched-on Gutenberg**;
>   accepted by **Spindrift**)

The lord's tweet

our dad up hi
U r super
yer wayz cool all over
give us bred 2day
4giv r breakins
we do & WTF no luring
Fedx evil away
u r very great
rule on
amen

    (published by **Mad Swirl**)

Missoula migration

Geese vee north into half-light,
slip through Montana sky.

We tromp damp riverbank,
follow the Clark Fork flow, peer

into coming night as the gaggle
sweeps by. I believe I see

a female veer off, gain speed,
slice past stragglers, take her turn

at the lead. I step in your tracks
while the setting sun bleeds.

    (published by **Third Wednesday**)

Missoula possums
(with a nod to Chuck Luckmann)

Mother bled out on rainy blacktop,
I rescue a dozen newborn

from cooling pouch, nestle them
deep in long hair behind my ears.

Their pink hands cling to my finger
as I feed them droppers of milk.

I sneak them to school, sit way back
in class, wool cap, off, on again

for warmth. My hair rustles.
Miss Prudence ignores, believes me

a child of hippies, with lice.
The possums grow, fill mouths

with teeth. Mom mashes dead flies,
carrots, peas. Possums trail behind

as I gather firewood, rake fall leaves.
Dad builds a shelter behind the yurt.

They return home to it each autumn,
vanish again early in the spring.

> (published by **Windfall**; different
> version published later in 2016 by
> **Third Wednesday** as "Possum rescue")

My last professor
(with a nod to Robert Browning)

There, see his portrait on the wall.
I believe him to be the exception,

not the rule. He lasted fall, winter,
almost till spring — persevered, gave,

shall I say, not just light,
but hope — inspired a bit of love

to begin. Then new semester —
classes in lit, stats, chem,

attraction ebbing, new interest,
same pattern — learning, powerful men.

Notice this photo, though, coup d'état,
prize-winning biology prof

making dissected frogs
jump high again.

    (published by **Carcinogenic Poetry**)

No mending love

Sun frayed by a million clouds,
zenith torn, tossed away,
her eyes suddenly gone
from green to ultramarine,

back to black, or so it seems.
Slipped away, her lithe sway,
whisper, smile, invitation
to stay awhile. Nirvana,

worn through, in need of mercy,
repair, a stitch or two.
Like leopard leap, kestrel dive,
my hushed heart gashed deep,

the wound so ragged, wide,
any seamstress mending love
would cease to sew, shove
needle aside, give up hope.

(published by **Kumquat Poetry Challenge**)

Not still water

Somewhere beyond darkness
it must be chiseled in porcelain

redemption sits just around
the corner, forgiveness there

not still water, but bubbling up,
spring gushing clean, like hope,

break of day, pristine,
a bright artesian bidet.

    (published by **The Curious Record**)

Past tents

Dream back how you waded
a Montana stream, at each bend
cast Brown-Bear-Blacks

toward the far bank. Until dusk.
Until cold crept in. Fire reflected gold
on meadow grass when you returned

to camp. Rainbows alive a few hours ago
sizzled in the skillet, red stripes
still bright on their sides. Outfished again,

you devoured her lithe form, half-lit
in shadows where she bent,
spatula in hand. Mint along the creek

sent sweet scent into gathering night.
Willows resisted wind, became
black pickets around your tent.

Full, the day spent, you were happy
to press against her back
as the moon rose and she slept.

(published by **Third Wednesday**)

Real man howls

Armpit hair with darkened curl
announces a soulful,

acoustic woman. Organic.
Escapee from brotherhood

of jockstrap. I sense hope
within black growth, believe

she might, indeed, be free —
doesn't love beauty contests,

riding horses, can make
a decent quiche — will teach me

how to knit, read Munro aloud,
show me how a real man howls.

> (published by **Toasted Cheese**)

Revolutions

Go for it, run in. Believe
they won't inch back, hold

rope too high — prevent whisk
on brick, force leaps,

not skips, whirled snake
biting ankle, shin, thigh.

Free will has a bit
to do with it. Judge height,

time right, not something
only the lucky achieve —

tripped up by hot peppers,
revolutions pelting toes, feet,

knees. Finally inside, hopping,
hoping, beginning to breathe,

rope gone slow, end coming —
the powerful changing speed.

    (published by **Clover, A Literary Rag**)

Second person

You're not the first to say,
*someday I'll go to sleep
and not wake up.*

Secretly hope you're wrong.
Merely sick, depressed a bit,
death-talking to yourself —

down a black path,
admired, coffined, tan.
Staring back handsome,

kissed, missed, gone. Wonder
if you had friends, listened,
cared, shared, cried —

a second chance, smooth ride
downhill, loved ones waving
goodbye, you, still inside.

(published by **Aberration Labyrinth**)

She-devil

Horoscopes torn out, read,
shared, but not with me.

Separate lives, serrated nights.
I'm in a tunnel, running,

the train surely coming —
not your breasts, not you.

I inhale fear, chest wide open,
heart cut half out, you,

the ripper. Or, so I feel.
Destined to lick sooty walls

re-painted black, I cannot
eat myself, puke life back.

Tonight, without light,
I lie flat on bleak track.

    (published by **Otoliths**)

Silenced night
(with a nod to Albert Camus)

I dream I reach out in darkness,
make a timid offering. Great joy
rises within me from knowing

I am desired. Pressed firmly
to cool canvas on the bottom
of a black tent, she strains upward

into fleeing night, trembles
as the stream goes quiet nearby,
later tries to calm her heart

though heat still overflows
in wave after wave. At dawn,
even the faintest stars slide lower

on the horizon and become still.

> (published by **Clover, A Literary Rag**;
> republished by **Windsor Review**

Swallow

I pop a chocolate chunk
into my mouth, bite through,

move it left, drain center goo.
I swallow the cherry brandy

sugar sweet, suck my cheeks.
Send what's left to roof, tongue

underneath. I savor the cocoa,
both eyes closed. Guilt dictates

this to be plain yogurt, fat-free,
not a seventy-percent evil treat.

> (published by **WWU Retirement News**)

Taut too

Wake at dawn, still high,
sheets a mess. Eyes closed,
lips pressed, roll over,

sigh — whirl toward sun, dream
black clouds, legs spread wide,
toes taut too. Pause mid-sky,

come down hard — splits doomed —
among cosmos, anemone,
hyacinth, lilies in bloom.

> (published by **Convergence**)

Texting the savior

U R pissd I C but revenge
can B served way 2 cold.

Was it the 30 coins thing
or becuz U were naild

2 the X? I no that hurts
Y now? They R ded

U got out, remember?
And Y the I'll B bak?

WTF, U shouldn't
cum bak just 2 get me.

      (published by **Aberration Labyrinth**)

Upgrading to poutine
at the Radium, B.C. bar & grill

A buck fifty extra to let salad slide,
have the french fries drenched in gravy —
white cheese curds layered tasteless

on its top. I'd order the evil treat
if crowned with ahi, not served alongside
a charred slab of Spam. Full, fingers

licked, I would also tip much better
if not expected to love hockey,
ice dancing, get excited about snow

or were not seated by a family
with crying babies — all of us far away
from the window with a great view

of the river, where Big Horn sheep
have heard of the dish, graze
in the meadow, put up tents,

sleep, dream of finding globs of it
by the restaurant's yawning dumpster
after they put on blush at dawn.

    (published by **Windfall**)

Vacuuming around the dead

Dirt finds a way to lie with remains —
casket open, deceased propped up,

lips purple, fine-lined, sewn tight,
eyes gray, dust layered on face.

Lights go bright, vacuum whines,
bristled brush swish, grime erased

like life. Chapel dim again, hose
stowed, lid closed, the cleansed,

sealed in. Filth, final ride, outside,
dumpster gaping on a moonless night.

(published by **Dual Coast Magazine**)

War memorial

No names are etched here.
The bomb-scarred wall
runs scared over the rise

then dives for cover.
Village ruins lie tangled
in vines — charred thatch,

broken bowls, human bones.
Stench no longer drifts in
from napalm spread on jungle

like bad jam. High in kapok trees,
pintail snipes sing of a child
who ran naked from flames

toward her white saviors.
They still hover over her
like fans on a hot night.

(published by **War, Literature & the Arts**)

Wrong a lot

Lake's plenty deep, dive off the cliff.
She's crazy about me. Those jeans
will fit. I'll be there for her

if the going gets tough. No chance
it will rain, I know when to shut up.
I don't need directions,

they adore me at work. I've studied
enough, no doubt I'll get rich.
We've got plenty of gas,

she doesn't want gifts. Our love
will survive, we don't need cash,
I'm sober, can drive. It's fine

to speed. I will never get caught.
I know she'll call, she wouldn't leave.
I won't miss her at all.

    (published by **Sue Boynton Poetry Contest**;
    republished by **Whatcom Watch**)

Yellowstone recital
(in memory of Sara Hulphers)

The dream, swim with friends,
Firehole River flowing black
as Old Faithful spews white geysers

toward stars somewhere east.
Maybe strip to panties, dive deep,
shiver together towel-wrapped

on the bank. No way to know
ribbon you leap in darkness
wraps a boiling pool, thin-crusted

for your landing. Splash, plunge.
Someone grabs scalded hair,
yanks you out. Steaming, you see

flesh ooze off arms, hands, know
you stand there dead. Before tingles
turn to bright pain, sobs

to screams, you recite goodbyes
to mother, brother, dad.
Hot tears cool when they land.

    (published in **Mapping water**)

Poems 2015

Another Bellingham Valentine's Day

Opposite ends, Boulevard Park bench,
lovers shiver, speak no words.

She texts mom; he orders chocolates
from Amazon. Hands jammed in pockets —

his into his, hers, hers — they blow kisses
then leave, driving scarlet SUVs.

Another park, across the bay, a surgeon mime
gives his quivering heart away.

   (published by **Bellingham Herald**)

Attuned to home

A rabbit lies flattened
on the highway side —

paws crossed, whiskers erect,
rear legs frozen in mid-stride.

Cottonwood fluff outlines
the rigid body fuzzy white.

Her dead eyes, glazed
brown as bark, search

for more big rigs headed west.
Ears point behind, intent,

no doubt listening for small cries
coming from her nest.

> (earlier version published
> by **WWU Retirement News**)

Bellingham limerick

She planned only green for the day,
even dyed her hair lime as a way
to show Irish sass
yet not be too crass —
subdued excitement on display.

> (published by **Bellingham Herald**)

Bituminous nightmare

Some horrors fade to black,
carry fear of ribboned trains away —
coal cars winding along the coast,

bituminous nightmare shoveled aside,
fiery crashes put out of mind.
Certainly, no dust settles by tracks,

on cedar, maple, alder, ash —
fine film on berries, children, grass.
No train snakes border to B.C. pier,

spews ebony lumps into cargo ships.
No silica blows down Salish Sea,
coats docks, boats, sails, masts.

No dust blankets bay, sinks deep,
turns sockeye red to charcoal gray.
No Lummi fisher paddles strait,

cremates empty, blackened net
on sable beach. In grimy sky,
no ragged vees of inky geese.

>   (published by **Windfall**; republished by
>   **Whatcom Watch**; *Mapping water*)

Capital love

She apologized for her affair,
confessed need to see

new men every year
or two or three,

asked tearfully for a metaphor.
He said love is a purple orchid

arcing down in morning sun
from high planter in solarium.

A wilted orchid.
Hanging at daybreak.

    (published by **Convergence**)

Fluke

We sleep molded, spooned in peace,
me behind, arm draped over side,

hand by breast, no longer locked,
damp, intense, sheets mussed,

lips pressed. Now, eyes closed,
each breath's easy flow, dream —

fortuitous love, happenstance,
magic, luck, fluke, like lying

amid jasmine, a whole field
swaying gold, then by chance, you,

lithe guide opening a slim path
for me to slip through.

   (published by **Poetry Quarterly**)

Gettysburg tweet

years back
ol dads got free
now big fite 2 endure
time out here
we cant equal the dead
so forget us
blah blah devotion
give it up 4 democracy

>   (published by **Mad Swirl**)

Hooking black sky

Sunset dollops fuchsia glaze along the bay
where city sludge oozes toward surf,

life contrasted on sand in the setting.
Light, like hope, refuses to die,

tosses up some gold as a one-armed mime
tries to hook black sky nearby.

>   (published by **Mad Swirl**)

I cannot do the splits

the way blonde cheerleaders
in mini-skirts land hard,
slap thighs at mid-court —

one leg out front, straight,
the other stretched back,
toes pointed, everything taut —

bounce back to their feet,
cartwheel around, five times
or four. Hope, however,

does leap up, seek bright sky,
gain height, write a love poem
on damp parchment, in Greek,

before coming down, janitor
once more, still dreamy,
to mop the gym floor.

    (published by **Mad Swirl**)

It's not nothing

No, it isn't,
never was not nothing,

not now, anyhow,
not anymore —

nor anyone important.
Anyway, never in life

has so much
not meant so little.

    (published by **The Curious Record**)

Letter from the Wolong Reserve

Panda mouths pink in China dusk
cast shadows on bamboo shoots
crushed to softness like fallen monks.

Savage Qionglai winds shake me awake
before I dream. It is rumored
panda males oppress. I don't believe it,

know females prefer to be alone
except when mating, black and white lives
spent curled in snow on winter nights.

At dawn, Wolong cold flails savage
at your memory, tests my love,
your choice — Seattle, damp, gray,

not Chengdu, outpost, me. Pandas
love bamboo, succumb to arrow sprouts
as bait, get trapped, hauled away, caged.

In rage, they mangle feeding bowls,
frantic, sniff despair in wind.
Someone must dream them home again.

(published by **The Curious Record**)

Lie at a slow pace

Coffins mired in mud,
we recline here, stuck,

unable to find traction,
churn along deep ruts,

get to where the road ends.
We hope someone comes

with a rope, hooks on,
drags us to higher ground,

does not see we have
one leg draped over the edge.

    (published by **Poetry Quarterly**)

Lilac moon

Lily blossoms sleep alone,
droop in pre-dawn dark,
touch briefly, then rise violet.

Each begins to open,
stretches in morning dew,
traces sun turning red to gold

making some brighter way
across a periwinkle day.
By dusk, like them,

we come together, bloom,
casting one lavender shadow
under a lilac moon.

(published by **WWU Retirement News**)

Little adobe something-or-other in Santa Fe
(with a nod to Alex Vouri)

If it does not work out, that dream
each time a lover leaves — buy

a fleet of taco trucks, nubile teens
working Seattle streets, then kick back

since you don't have a goddamn thing
to worry about — one option would be

hitchhike southwest, roll out your bag
in dark desert, lie face up,

inhale moon, the whole Milky Way,
actually wake at sunrise,

explore arroyos, red cliffs, ruins
more important than your life,

inhale smoke from burning sage,
breathe deep, get a meaningful job,

save your pay, buy a little adobe
something-or-other in Santa Fe.

(published by **Cirque**)

Lucky

I awake listless each day, rise
but don't smile, never kick sky, play —

pretend it is fine no one sleeps
by my side. I say I deserve nothing,

live miserly on surprise. I lie.
When I trudge dark passages, ignore

every full moon, hear dour chords,
stomp roses in full bloom, I actually fan

the flame of love by not having any.
Nobody knows of this hope to get lucky —

a soulmate arrives with smoldering eyes.
I weep from relief, sing — and, yes, sigh.

(published by **The Kumquat Poetry Challenge**)

Mapping water

Call it Salish Sea, river,
stream. Leaves float side

by side, touch briefly
in some ripple, drift off,

too often face down.
Absent leaves are called

lost, deceased, the dead —
names unable to capture

fading of green to brown,
ensuing brittleness, struggle

not to go under, lose sight
of day, slide to the bottom,

lie motionless there, decay.
We hope all the leaves

have not vanished, buds
are on the way, more water

waits for mapping.
Faith rises from the belief

we still have enough time
to cast about for a new spring.

> (published by **Third Wednesday**;
> republished in *Mapping water*)

Mourning becomes eclectic

Call it the spawning of grief.
Brother, enemy, mother, niece,

dad, sister, cousin, friend —
deceased, all but memories gone.

Lover too on the run, vanished, lost,
no longer fondled, kissed.

Spouse of abuse, absent — bruises,
weirdly, also missed. All the beloved

mourned like unsung hymn, lost limb,
stolen gun, burned-out sun.

   (published by **Carcinogenic Poetry**)

Night-blooming cereus

This flower wafts memory back to me
as I dream another for you.

Paired in darkness, blossoms droop,
rise separately, petals tinged violet,

filled with midnight dew,
never trace red sun turned gold

nor explore day's full bloom.
Alone, together, dampened by night,

they open, spread wide briefly,
cast a single lilac shadow — then

exude sweet fragrance and die
under a billowing moon.

>   (published by **WWU Retirement News**)

No giving up

So what if he melts wedding ring,
removes tattoos, culls photo album —
as if she remains the indelible center

of existence, cause for end of day,
dour reason to text the savior,
gut all hope, breathe snow,

unsmell her scent, make bucket list,
smudge life, not do the splits.
It could be he plans redemption —

gain enough grace to repaint souls,
eat bitter hearts, force-feed geese,
put gray doves of peace to sleep —

with luck, make each day a blessing,
joyful chance to explode mosquitos,
count ravens, zigzag mow,

herd flies, do gravestone math,
vacuum cats, circle ruins on a map —
at sunset, six nightmares late,

fence in darkness, recite night sky,
dream all the blackness
back to light.

(published in ***Whatcom Writes Anthology***;
republished in ***Mapping water***)

Out of Missoula
"The fear is always there. If you return home
 you risk madness."
     — Richard Hugo,
     The Real West Marginal Way

I drive away lost, again —
parents dead, lover gone —
follow the Clark Fork down,
wend my way west, Montana

to coast, Puget Sound hook of sand
where chum salmon begin,
later end Dungeness River run.
Unlike me, they learn early to breathe,

filter hope from salt, avoid hook,
barb, net. I suck sea air in,
exhale Missoula, gray snow, ice.
I wade angry surf, empty my mind,

face into fierce wind, feel its sting
rip ribs even as it picks
beach logs clean. Everything here
needs to be punished. Cleansed white,

redeemed. Reason enough
to trade gray for gray, tithe life —
lie face up in foam, madness
busy stripping human bones.

  (published by **San Pedro River Review**;
   republished in ***Mapping water***)

Packing tattoos

Nudes sprawl in the second drawer
way back behind sheets,

roses, in boxes on closet shelf,
dragons, swirled red, purple, green,

in black tub under bed, lid on tight.
Mother lies in the high cupboard, alone.

Moon, stars are tucked below, locked
with skulls, hearts, lethal snakes.

No resting place exists for your name,
seven letters being an awkward size —

no easy fit for ordinary containers —
taking up too much or too little space.

I plan to wear it home with me
after filling in my grave.

    (published by **Convergence**)

Reciting night sky

Name one of the stars in Orion's belt.
Clever responses to lover's test

lodge in throat, no way to whisper wrongly,
Penelope, Andromeda, Cassiopeia —

even Mintaka, correct guess, stuck,
proof of being no good at sky,

only dippers, big, little, both holding nothing,
empty as a midnight street,

or a Sunday morning boast — *finished,
week's most difficult crossword puzzle,*

again, with a bad hangover, in pen —
both dippers tipped back so hope runs out,

flows along the curb toward dawn.
Time to cross blacktop alone, count stars

on the other side, faintest ones first,
maybe find peace at eight hundred and five.

(published by **Tipton Poetry Journal**)

Salt over the left shoulder

Fleur de sel — to set the bar —
not so much for show,

more, belief the good stuff
will provide flavored certainty

of luck. Avoid tossing over right,
in case holy investigations

bring superstitious truth
to light. It's a matter

of taste, karma, free will —
another day to live, to spill.

    (published by **Hobo Pancakes**)

Scattering ashes at Squalicum Beach
(in memory of Anne Andreasen)

Friends drift in on wind,
recall her independence,

imagine her smile returning,
surging with high tide. They know

even now she won't be owned,
believe she will rise to greet them

so they hum a song of hope.
Sisters carry shrouded ash —

charred end after a long battle —
endure dawn chill, begin the goodbye.

Their collective breath dives deep,
pauses vacant, still, but not lost.

Tossed aloft, she dances again,
a small gray cloud spiraling in mist.

Butterflies, purple, gold, white,
sweep by, flit upward into clearing sky.

(published by **Labyrinth**)

Second Coming expert

So you died at the wheel,
drifted to side of road,

Porsche coming to a halt
because your heart had stopped.

A homeless man walking by
gave you mouth to mouth,

thumped chest, brought back life.
Some are not so sure

this rescue was a good thing,
given the tendency now to preach,

your repeated reminder
of rising from the dead —

no fish or loaves handed out,
but saying which gluten-free bread

to eat. And cut down on red meat
and cheese. Also, stay away

from fries, chips, cake, pie —
at tunnel end, there may not be

a passerby, lolling hooded,
lonely, heeding every cry.

(published by **Electric Windmill Press**)

Summer maid

Sommelier, one who tastes,
likely from old French,

a pack animal driver.
Imagine Provence, late July,

lavender field, lovers, picnic,
checked sheet spread out,

morbier cheese, red wine,
baguette, not a soul nearby,

nibble, sip, dip, sleep.
Sommelier, proud noun,

not sommelied, some verb,
dreary, listless way to eat.

> (published by **Carnival**; republished
> in *Carnival Poetry Anthology*)

Tent not taken

Salish Sea inked black below,
teated mountains, staggered rows,

summits frozen, dolloped white,
raw wind wild down ragged slopes,

backdropped stars put out by night.
Campfire cold, hunched alone,

love charred, memory iced, tent
cloaked in snow. Time to creep inside,

breathe out the light, dream of sleep
or try to try.

   (published by **Tipton Poetry Journal**)

Traitor Joe

Be assured, not an easy task, even aided
by fine wine, a Côtes du Rhône —

in fact, I did not actually plant the wheat,
grind flour, sift it, grow greens,

force-feed geese, take their livers,
make foie gras from scratch,

hors d'oeuvre served with cornichons
prior to our main course, coq au vin,

for which I had hunted mushrooms,
slaughtered a hog, killed my cock.

I did, however, drive the Porsche
to a trendy market, spend much time,

find these delicacies, endure checkout,
pass it all off to you as mine.

    (published by **Carcinogenic Poetry**)

Poems 2014

Bellingham Caesar

Roam Holly Street, search out
wooden bowl, bamboo spoons.
Press garlic cloves, at least three,

grab lemon tight, squeeze, squeeze,
pour juice in, then add dijon —
a heaping spoon of Maille

or Grey Poupon. Pepper, black,
just a pinch, coarse, ground,
two of salt, slosh around.

Worcestershire splashed,
four anchovies mashed,
stir the golden, chunky mix

then drizzle olive oil in,
whirl, swirl, make sauce thick.
Romaine lettuce, Northwest grown,

green, washed, spun desert dry,
ripped by hand to bite-size chunks,
no pallid leaves, no bulky stems,

toss together, add grated cheese —
Parmesan, Pecorino among the best —
top with avocado if you please.

Eat this Caesar when subdued,
after meal, in peace, yes last,
as is done in southern France.

(earlier version published in **Bellingham Poems**)

Candle rescue

Long after rogue match spits fire,
gives slender candle light,

burning high then low,
wax somehow finds a way

to pool, drown flicker, flame,
make candle yearn to cease to glow.

Save the light — single hole knifed
in softened edge, hot wax

sent aflow down candle side
brings dying wick back to life.

(published by **WWU Retirement News**)

Dregs

Spread out Syrah noir wide, slide up
wine glass side, stick in patterns

to the edge, like leftover phrases, words
lining the darkened bottom

of a writing drawer. Try to read
some kind of future in the tailings,

see a story finally done,
were there light enough, or life,

or snowy woods, or hawks
finding wind to soar and dive.

Well, maybe one more glass,
no past, no looking back,

a bottle, two, alone, black sky —
hope, the only ending, no you.

    (published by **Mad Swirl**)

Exploding mosquitos

Imagine her your lover
who cheats, repeats, lies.

Just before goodbye, offer
a bare arm. As she drills,

begins to fill, clench fist tight
then hold. Taut muscles grip

like a vice, trap proboscis.
Unable to break free, no spigot

to stop flow, her belly expands,
turning maroon as it grows.

Your heartbeat alone
will make her explode.

> (published by **Poetry Quarterly**;
> shorter version published in 2013
> by **Three Line Poetry**)

Fab Four failure

Ruined. August concert at the city park —
outdoor music billed as Beatles night,

just *Seventeen, Nowhere Man, Yesterday*,
twangy blue-grass rendition of Fab Four hits

bringing dancers to a halt, any urge
to kick skyward, gone, all whirl vanished,

frozen, standing there, soaking up dew,
every wool cap drooping with disgust

while John Bob weaves, Ringo washboards,
Pauline saws stand-up bass, Geo fiddles

and only five-year-olds who know no better
boogie wildly on the damp grass

as if this were the best tribute ever,
better even than Purple Haze redux,

highlight last year by Snoose Gone Loose,
whoop-ass finale to the county fair.

    (published by **Poetry Quarterly**;
    republished in ***Bellingham Poems***)

Fire licks the canyon rim

A vision, she arrives with power,
like desert lightning over Grand Canyon,
five miles wide, nearly as deep.

At dawn, he begs her to lie with him,
wildflowers spreading out like red clover
from her hair, bright smile.

She touches heels together,
one foot pointed away toward sage,
scrub oak, Ponderosa pine,

cliff offering pieces of shale
to the Colorado snaking silent
from the night. She points the other

toward him, permits morning sun
to highlight her green eyes,
turn them Yaqui yellow,

bring the whole plain to life,
make it throb with heat.
They dream of the coming moon,

two smoldering as one
under dappled sky. It is then
fire licks the canyon rim.

(published by **Windfall**)

Forced feeding

Your long hose snakes down from a vat
filled with moist corn. Hungry geese
gather like elfers around an eel
or politicians, a lobbyist feast.

Coax one close, lock her with knees,
lift head, stretch neck taut like rope
or string. Shove your hose
past puckered bill, down closed throat —

open spigot, corn blasts out
a golden stream. Giddy,
she staggers off, foie gras full,
dreaming of the next great meal.

    (published by **Public Republic**)

Full creel at sunset

He circles the campfire, giddy,
waves a string of dead fish,
does not think to question why
currents center, then pool.
She creeps off, listens to sparks

from the darkest shadows,
watches embers go black,
sink into gray ash. After a time,
he sees her gasping, as if in a creel.
She pictures herself bleeding deep.

    (published by **Poetry Quarterly**)

Gestapo glaciers

Like climate change,
they did not come quickly
but were relentless and ruthless,
nonetheless — with their share

of disbelievers, along with those
who saw beauty in the way

they inched over lives with ice.

    (published by **Mad Swirl**)

Hawking holy books

They roam rundown Bronx streets,
student Christians working on the cheap,
lay out black Bibles on green felt,
plead with men slurping beer —

buy one, put us through seminary,
two, rescue children overseas,
three, save a family in Tibet,

build hospital, send kids to school —
church raffle tickets too — first prize,
New York-New York suite in Vegas,
buffet, poker chips, a show —

maybe discount Bible software,
with free dashboard savior,
head bobbing as up he goes.

    (published by **Hobo Pancakes**)

Horses, whiskey, ropes

People back East discuss politics.
Folks here talk robberies, wrecks,
gossip about neighbors, lovers,
tell jokes. Cowboys talk
horses, whiskey, ropes.

>   (published by **Hobo Pancakes**)

Hot

If I say often *it's boiling, burning, hot —*
will you not touch with fingers, lips, tongue?
Unless it is me, then, yes, you must.

>   (published by **Three Line Poetry**)

If a tree falls

in deep forest, no one around,
will any sound — whoosh, snap,
crash, thunk — be heard?

Puzzle locked in question
handed down, old man limps
past trailhead, camps,

last mountain bike busy buzz,
beyond loggers, heads bent,
saws slashing pine and fir,

leaves behind winding stream
where fishers whip sky
with line and flies, tempt

cutthroat lying deep to rise.
He finds one tamarack
standing tall in silent death,

corpse, yet wooden monument —
with ax, beavers vee deep
in tree's downhill side,

leaves pack, retreats past stream,
logs, saws, finds camp, tent,
sleeps in night wind, dreams.

Faint path traced back at dawn,
pack, near tamarack fallen down —
on tape recorder, a crashing sound.

(published by **Still Crazy**)

If hope were a shriek in the night

and we heard it in spring wind,
saw it in the distance as we wheeled
from Seattle for a long weekend
with lover at Omak, smelled it

in towns we drove by, got a glimpse
amid roadside wheat desiring more sun
in sky not all that pale yet wishing
itself were a shade deeper blue,

we'd sense it oozing in veins
past clots ready to break loose,
collect in brains only yearning
for longer life, not seeking revenge

for years and years of grease
sopped up with fresh bread,
having forgotten vows never to wipe
bacon drippings from plates again —

and, maybe finally, touch it,
trace it on lover's thigh
in desperate, periwinkle pulsing,
making us anything but shy —

last chance to be revered
under silk Omak sheets,
where, moved by relief, not lust,
we would shriek, not cry.

(published by **Cirque**)

Life benedict

Dawn, a bit down,
stopped by this morning,
hoping to catch a ride to night,

found us as usual running late,
in need of speed, luck, good lights
just to make noon on time.

Plus, it's no good, codependent,
enabling patterns of friends
who find a way to intrude on life.

Maybe, listen, try to smile,
offer eggs, not a ride,
with hollandaise, sunny side up.

> (published by **WWU Retirement News**)

Love that operates

Surgeons stroll together, poodle
prancing behind, lust after sailboats

vying for position on the windy lake,
shiver in silence on opposite ends

of a sullen bench. She texts her mom;
he yawns. They order new scalpels

from Amazon. Patients hide
amid shale, wait for wind to die.

Pompom must be about to freeze.
She agrees, tugs the leash,

rises to leave. They shuffle back
to matching SUVs, without words,

hands jammed into pockets,
his into his, hers into hers.

(published by **Hobo Pancakes**)

Mercy-killing marriage

Avoid a taxable event. Keep iPad,
laptop, diamond rings.

Give her Kindle, china, SUV —
silver, vintage albums,

especially Sting. Take dog, boat,
football seats. Yield lakeside home,

mountain cottage, beach retreat.
Keep condo, IRA, hidden gold.

Share children, friends — yes,
makes it equal, even neat.

You pay her health club dues;
she pays your attorney's fee.

(published by **Mad Swirl**)

One-mime town
(with a nod to Dean Wright)

In Boulder, Missoula, Santa Fe —
not Shiloh, Duluth, Butte, Dubuque —

mimes blow up clear balloons,
draw back bows, take aim,

let feral boomerang arrows go,
belly-crawl out whitewashed holes,

fall three floors, mouth screams to crowd,
become carpool-tunnel-syndrome clowns

driving up imagined waterfalls, not down.
Mimes abandoned in darkened towns

pray alone in some strip-mall church
then plunge to death off a pew-side curb.

(published by **Mad Swirl**)

Oregon Coast rainbow birthing

Clouded dusk, sun on the go,
I look up from waves to see

an unexpected rainbow
inside another — mirrored golds

purples, forest greens
reaching up from underneath.

I cease to breathe,
hope to see yet one more,

emerging tiny, mostly pink,
nuzzling for a bit of sky

before, like shrouded sun,
vanishing into hungry night.

    (published by **WWU Retirement News**)

Orphan
(for Pete Steffens)

Mother, father, both gone, dead,
two truths emerge for any children left.
One, you are an orphan. Two, you are next.

    (published by **Convergence**)

Out of control

He thought when he died
his lover would swoon,

believe all hope to be lost
then dutifully die too.

Photos — placed on mantel,
cat-sunning ledge, next to bed —

grayed from dust. Old Spice scent
faded from sofa, pillow, rug.

Puppy chewed his urn,
carried ashes room to room,

gnawed bits of bone,
yellowed copies of his poems.

Not all sway vanished, went away —
he's the password on her phone.

    (published by **Still Crazy**)

Reliving Vietnam at the Dillon, Montana, class reunion

"Are not our lives too short for that full utterance
which through all our stammerings is of course
our only and abiding intention?"
— Joseph Conrad in **Lord Jim**

Seniors of 1965 had dreams,
professed faith in country,
some in God, but we all prayed
no draft, no war, no death.
We believed choosing

made lives lived half-right, not worthless.
I remember Gary Dumke, hulking, obese,
Piggy in our small Montana town
with flies, no Simon, no lord.
Football coaches wanted Gary on the line,

lured, cajoled, made him turn out.
I watched him practice in rain,
weep alone after Saturday games.
Gary found courage enough to say no —
walked away, retired helmet, cleats,

ignored jeers, dressed in tie and suit,
carried briefcase, joined debate.
I recall senior government class,
Mr. Claudius Ankeny, Army veteran,
paddle-toter to the core

saying, *Gary, you look nice today.*
Gary ripped my breath away,
responded in no-first-name taboo,
Why thank you, Claude.
Pure surprise made Claudius freeze,

spared Gary punishment, hands
grabbing ankles as hickory board
spat blisters on his three-piece behind.
Graduation past, Gary stood tall again.
Dillon's draft board ordered him

turn out, fight in Nam.
He dressed in tuxedo, boarded train,
then hanged himself,
swinging free above dutiful draftees
sweating their way to war.

    (published by **Trestle Creek Review**)

Table-side magic

Ocean view, gourmet cafe,
tiny tables, chairs back to back,
Raoul swoops in, cape aswirl,

snaps fingers — candles light.
He strokes young blonde's hair,
coins emerge, four then five.

Teal doves fly out one sleeve,
beak some bread, peck at brie,
become small eggs on salad greens.

Locked pepper handcuffs drop
from lights. Presto — slices intertwined,
yellow, red. Volunteer brought on stage,

shut in box, drum-roll, tense scene —
Raoul saws lovely radish in half,
vanishes as she screams.

    (published by **Carnival**)

Things are well and going good

Actually, not true.
Life has turned into a fraudulent adverb

faking its way to death,
disguised as a successful modifier,

say, an adjective or gangly participle
with a whole covey of obedient followers.

As for going good, the well is —
how to put it — also a lie,

contains nothing of substance, has dried up —
redundantly and figuratively speaking.

After all, cisterns dry downward,
water slipping stealthily away

into gray clay, seeking black cracks
at shaft bottom, every drop,

like hope, vanished —
gone, well, forever, good.

    (published by **Public Republic**)

Toasting the city of subdued excitement

Let's drink to Bellingham, laid-back, low-key.
Opinions never spewed, just tapped out slowly,

gentle caress of keys, written lowly,
dreamy reasoned stance Face-booked on PCs

or sent from iPhones by the meek.
Blue, placid bay, tide in two times a day,

even-tempered town spread out wide and green,
peaceful homes, snow-capped Baker rarely seen.

Where wind trades bits of sun for sullen gray,
at ease as clouded sky drips buckets of rain

while languid, peaceful lovers strive for bliss,
and say, *you look so succulent today.*

Bellinghamsters, so subdued, nothing amiss —
they kiss then spoon the night away.

    (earlier version published in **Bellingham Poems**)

Too much gossamer

When they finally cleaned out
the thirty-gallon coffee urn

used years by sleepy students
streaming through the cafeteria,

they found at the bottom
five inches of insect wings —

butterflies, moths, wasps, bees —
gossamer layer upon layer

packed tightly together
resisting filtration. Learning

never again tasted
so light, so free.

>   (published by **Cirque**; shorter version
>   published later in 2014 by **Three Line Poetry**)

Warning

This poem contains images
known in the State of California
to cause hope, wonder
and sometimes ability to think —

maybe even glimpse a sleek symbol
rising from metaphors to the east.
In Utah, it is known
to cause no dawn.

(published by **Electric Windmill Press**)

Wheelchair Warrior

Metro stop, fall morning,
mist turned cold. Lummi elder,
hair sprinkled like Baker snow,

sits silent, proud, wheelchair
his private reservation now.
Dutiful daughter, Limps in Life,

fights warrior's chair, bus lift
waiting to swoop the old man up.
Moccasins skid on damp tread, slip,

fail to grip. Headband, green,
red, dripped with sweat,
she retreats, admits defeat.

White riders hate these scenes,
frown, stare the driver down.
Eyes demand, *take control,*

forget them both, leave, go.
Wheelchair Warrior spins away,
reaches down, hugs Limps in Life.

She kneels, sobs. Bus seventy-five,
call it Fading Spirit,
whooshes into waiting fog.

(published in ***Bellingham Poems***)

Yes, yes, oh, yes

At night she walks her restless cat
on leather leash down black streets

then back, past motels, clubs, shacks,
lets it prowl nighttime sounds —

rat scratch, dog growl, piss splash,
drunk words slurred, slow drum beat,

lover's moan, a few high screams.

    (published by **Mad Swirl**)

Zigzag mowing

June almost gone, rain vanished too,
clover spread across the lawn,

bees swoop blooms — land, explore,
legs pollened before they go. Woeful task,

mowing grass, if one guides frantic moths
back to night, sets bathtub spiders

free outside, lets sugar ants form long lines.
How to proceed — creep, pause, weave,

zigzag mow, no chopping bees —
save each worker for the queen.

    (published by **WWU Retirement News**;
    republished in ***Bellingham Poems***)

Part professor, part poet

Poems arranged alphabetically by year:

    2013 pages 221-244
    2012 pages 245-272
    2011 pages 273-308
    2010 pages 309-332
    2000-09 pages 333-360

Poems 2013

Anemone

Rich in meaning, permit me
to spell her out for you —

flower watered by tears,
coming fully endowed into Greek,

daughter of wind
with a round, proud name.

White, tinged blue, purple,
red. *Ah nem oh nee.*

Only by naming can I breathe
any syllable, taste her beauty,

hope, murmur — maybe
take her home with me.

    (published by **Cirque**)

Breathing snow
(with a nod to Pete and Christina Dale)

You can do it awhile. Air pockets remain,
locked around ice crystals. But not forever —
just long enough to replay the avalanche

rolling over life, sweeping love downhill,
leaving you flattened in white,
no way to reach for sky. If your ears still hear,

eyes are not frozen closed, hand trapped
near face can clear a bit of space,
you may have sufficient time

to listen for swish of metal probes
slicing nearby, promising beams of light.
If tempted to sleep, imagine

a new lover finds you, scoops a place
by your side, lies close. Together,
you breathe hope into deep snow.

>(published by **Sue Boynton Poetry Contest**;
>republished by **Thick With Conviction**;
>*Bellingham Poems*; *Poetry Walk:*
>*The Second Five Years*; *Mapping water*;
>**Poetry Pacific**; **Better Than Starbucks**;
>**River Poets Journal**)

Cast away at Larrabee Beach

Not father or friend, you overhear
young mother's cell-phone confession,
sins whispered to Puget Sound surf —
absolution an afterthought

when she hurried west,
jumped a whole nation,
left lover to reclaim her baby
now sleeping shaded on the sand.

No hint how original separation came.
Pain, she murmurs, *erases memories* —
perhaps, someday, yours.
You wonder about her lover,

if she would re-recant,
follow him again, Florida,
Bermuda, maybe the Keys.
You guess her answer,

baby snuggled close, tiny fingers
curled around her breast,
sun-baked smile telling
precisely where love lies —

your own lover, gone astray,
offering no surf confession —
and you, no baby, double cursed,
cast away.

    (published by **Labyrinth**;
    republished in ***Bellingham Poems***)

Centering

I'm in some black shop,
building a coffin for my lover.

Each upright must be perfect,
bubble in the level centered

between red lines — steady,
middle of storm, moon full,

exactly midnight, current gone
in deep pool, stopped at the middle,

dark, still, cool. Casket lid
must be aligned, fit tight —

able to shut out the past,
a whole stream of memories.

Painted onyx, deadline late June,
wide enough for two.

    (published by **Farthermost Dream**)

Dweeb scarfs down yellow thing on a stick

Not corn dog skewered nor mustard shrimp,
impaled nonetheless — saffron treat

bought hot, black van, mid-block,
downtown, busy street. Not one clue

who dweeb is, his Facebook page,
where he lives. No redemption takes place,

no hate erased. Yet yellow glob gone,
dweeb too, with iPhone, poof,

head down, thumbs busy, thorny crown,
up dark alley in gold Subaru.

    (published by **Hobo Pancakes**)

The end

is near — actually, a ways off —
but close to beginning, premonition

in its own right to coda, finis, finish.
With luck, it will be a good day —

pinnacle, climax, crescendo —
having nothing to do with aftermath.

    (published by **The Curious Record**)

Faint memories of a beekeeper's daughter

In good time, she said, promise
stretched out in summer days
as I mowed Montana hay.
She cooked, served lunch,
denim sky, alfalfa field.

August near end,
autumn college days ahead,
purple buds laid low in rows,
she kept her word,
hid from dad behind white hives,

rode with me into yellow sky.
I did not know bees arrived
Fresno-fresh every spring —
worked all summer,
saw hope expire, honey stolen,

death pro quo —
no queen kept, winters alone.
When she calls, I whisper,
my head buzzing
as I lie by the phone.

    (published by **Windfall**)

Gerunds running down my leg

First, verbs began to collide,
in novels, no less. It was clear
the English Department running

the universe should assert itself.
Hope for writing no longer lay
in prepositions, slender adjectives

and strappingly comely adverbs
marching like linguists
toward a rigid master language —

erect, proud, but accidentally,
on occasion, flaccid, surely predicting
very many adverbs more. Then,

participles, multiplying like termites,
eating life out of whole sentences,
lolling about with infinitives —

themselves claiming to be verbs,
weasels trying to reject all nounhood —
brought total impotence to sonnets,

villanelles, even three-act plays.
Swaying over the blank hole of verse,
I felt gerunds running down my leg.

(published by **Trestle Creek Review**)

Grim reaper

Stuff of executioner, what
makes her tick?

Steady hand, piercing gaze —
iced lemonade in veins?

Does she dream of home,
children, relaxing run,

garden beans, morning sun?
Begin to cry

as she beheads
serial killer, former lover,

enemy of state? Or,
toss hood aside, text fate,

drive her hybrid, naked,
past graveyards at night, late?

    (earlier version published by **Convergence**)

Higgs Boson particle

It matters — and anti-matters.
We got the universe wrong

then physicists smoked good stuff,
dreamed up boson, gave others work

playing a lifetime with colliders.
We missed the cosmic speedway

dragging particles yon, hither,
failed to see celestial molasses

sticks the universe together.
Forever, we focused on twos:

evil, good; virgin, whore;
yes, no; less, more;

win, lose; hoarded, used —
should have turned off-brains on,

gambled, thought big, in fours:
night, dawn, day, dusk;

yes, sometime, maybe, no;
head to war, greet death,

decay in meadow,
wake up to snow.

(published by **Electric Windmill Press**)

Hoarding

As youth begins to die, title every empty list,
List. Send what's left of you down

for jars of pickles neat in rows,
gherkins hidden deep in the basement

past stacks of sacks of beans. Your life
may not be totally over yet,

so live on the cautious side — fill the tub
with water, along with empty jugs

that held cranberry, milk, apple, bleach.
It's okay now to dip into those preserves;

after all, their name permitted hoarding —
pears, peaches, beans, beets,

anything but kale, good only for torture,
stretched naked on the rack, tempting you

to squeeze the goddamn life out of it.
But now is not a time to let imagined lovers

take the day off. Pray for extra help
dragging the limp extension cord

to your neighbor's throbbing generator,
hoping she'll let you plug it in.

(published by **Electric Windmill Press**)

Ken Burns effect

I'm writing by candlelight in my tent,
next one over from Odysseus,

journey going on eight years,
nearly forever. Each day

we scan the sea, look leagues east,
almost back to Troy. The men mutter

we should be home now,
complain about the weather,

want more wine, more sheep.
They fear our next adventure

will be worse than Cyclops, Sirens.
If gods were filming this voyage for PBS,

they would likely zoom out,
show campfires, beached boats,

the whole island hopeless,
gauzy mist covering all light,

pan to one side, there in darkness,
Penelope, alone, unraveling night.

>(published by **Poetry Quarterly**; republished
>in *Noisy Water: Poetry from Whatcom
>County, Washington*; *Mapping water*;
>**Harbinger Asylum;** prose version, "Ken Burns
>Effect, the early years," published in 2020
>by **Cascadia Weekly**)

Martha's Cafe

Weeds stretch high in the parking lot.
Windows are boarded, doors sealed tight,
peeled strips of white paint flutter
like flags of failure in the wind.

This is George, Washington,
halfway between Montana and the Pacific.
Truckers don't venture off the freeway anymore,
intent on cherry pie wives deny in Glendive,

Missoula, Butte. Farmers don't leave combines
running outside, sit, bellies on counter,
sip coffee, fib about being rich, single
to the slim waitress who calls them *Hon*.

Martha's gone now, trading George
and miles of empty sky, promises,
bed behind the diner, for Mount Vernon,
new lover called Lucky, cop in control

of chance, hope arriving with each red light.
I'm driven to stop here ten times a year,
pull off I-90 at midnight, take pot-holed road
to cafe remains, let my rig idle outside,

feel decay whip mistakes into bad memories,
see dust devils circle nothing in moonlight.
Kenworth pointed west, I wish the past back,
dream of forgiveness, perform my ritual.

By dome light, I write poems on napkins
for Martha and her pie. Some trip soon,
I won't stop, just roll by, phone for help,
at least reach out — send a firm warning,

one about obsession: If you leave by three
for Mount Vernon, drive like hell,
you still cannot hope to deliver
a truckload of sonnets by dawn.

   (published by **Trestle Creek Review**)

Minoan moment

Crete, summer, sun, beach,
blondes near concession tent
ignore heat, debate bikinied

breast to breast. Hot sand
burning feet, they fidget,
shift weight, wipe away sweat

as each lays out her version
of a man-free world.
Points made shushed, not loud,

first one, then the other, turns,
pulls damp bottom loose
from cheeks burned bright,

sways slowly to her towel,
sexy stroll the important thing.
Vendor guy grins, spits,

tongs up another dog,
so red, so juicy,
so big it splits.

    (published by **Mad Swirl**)

Not alone
(with a nod to Alexander Solzhenitsyn)

B.C. camping, two of us, one tent,
lake nested below nippled peaks,
we watch dusk-sun
play out across water rippled

by fleeing geese. They zigzag upward
in frenzied rush to join
three half-formed vees
cutting through faded light.

We scan horizon to horizon,
see geese dot the entire sky —
nine rise in the east,
five lift off west,

eight more flap out of mist,
each faint cry echoing fear
they won't link up,
but will fly solitary into night.

On impulse, you stir our fire,
send up sparks, smoke, hope,
spiraling to guide their ragged lines.
I find a log in growing dark,

toss it on embers but fail to notice
the wood is alive
with ants. Desperate, they rush out,
scurry along the top.

We quickly roll the log on its side
so most can drop unburned
onto cool sand. Safe,
they turn, circle, circle

then climb back to their home.
They dance farewell brightly —
tiny orange torches — together,
not alone.

    (published by **The Curious Record**)

On guard

Trouble with partners nowadays,
number two, three, seven, eight,

is suspicion, agonizing wait —
likelihood each new lover,

who clearly has no flaws,
will become the old.

We scan life for patterns:
patio stroll, text sent, shut phone;

smile, blush, gaze too long;
business trip alone, panties gone;

friend's snicker, whisper, hiss.
Other than this vigil —

disguised with smiles, kisses —
new mates would be perfect,

not keep us awake, fearful
it is only love they fake.

(published by **Hobo Pancakes**)

On my gravestone

For the name, use Helvetica,
italic, seventy-two point, that's an inch tall,

big enough mourners won't need to squint.
Not minute like movie credits for gaffer,

best boy, stuntman, where my life was shot.
Make me fit on one line, not surname alone,

first name carved below — like life
cut in half, both parts falling empty

as happens with severed heads
and hearts. When I lived must be smaller,

say half inch, with wide space between lines
so that drivel fills the headstone.

Please do not capitalize every letter,
in effect, shouting to cemetery gardeners,

here lies an important man, show respect,
be slow to weed, water, mow.

Old lovers especially will appreciate
my life being chiseled in lower case.

> (published by **Electric Windmill Press**;
> republished in ***Mapping water***)

Posse of angels

They gather at dusk in rain,
ready for the chase — not being saved,

apparently, out of the question —
proudly proclaim many angels

are celestial beings of color,
an appropriate number, for sure.

Plus, the whole posse, gender-balanced,
including a few who flit back

and forth. Several have only one wing,
or are known to fly a crooked line.

A number cannot hear any prayer.
Some have Tourette's. A few are blind.

Yet they are all angels,
equally able to hunt outlaw souls.

Tracked, caught, tied, this is on
a pamphlet they nail to my chest.

They are buoyed by their success —
I am bound to be blessed.

> (published by **The Curious Record**;
> republished in ***Mapping water***)

Quid pro quo

Wasps lie in wait, ambush fruit flies
near ripening peaches, plums, grapes.

They inject prey with eggs —
not by using stingers.

Baby wasps within, feeding on them,
the flies buzz off, woozy, beeline it

to nearest brandy snifter,
slip over the rim, crawl down in,

sip a bit, swim. They know alcohol
kills drunks, politicians, and wasps.

One whiff of good stuff will do. Some flies
hang out in a Hennessy glass for hours

on pretense of ridding themselves of wasps.
Rumor has it Iranians are training brigades

of fruit flies. To counter this threat,
wasps in formation have been seen

careening low over Los Alamos,
egg guns sewn to gossamer wings.

    (published by **Farthermost Dream**)

Six ounces late

Clock hands stand at nine miles —
no way to know how many grams pass

before my time. Yet I am optimistic,
bask Celsius in shadows of deceased,

believe kilometers, not mere feet,
tick through veins, surge down arteries,

arrive at a heart several metric tons deep.
I am prepared to vacuum ash-filled souls

into endless infinities of somethingness,
spurt happiness over a three-pint universe,

spew forth boxed sets of five-liter lives.
Hopeful, brined giddy, full of Fahrenheit,

I weigh in, time existence, measure fate.
As expected, death is six ounces late.

(published by **Farthermost Dream**)

Smudging

Pick Bon Accord sage fresh at dawn,
still damp from dew.
Dry it flat in sun, gray spray

spreading like moth wings,
purple buds bulged, clouds above
gathering for their own ceremony.

Meditate until evening.
Focus on why your life needs smudging.
Include cruel words, lies,

lovers, friends tossed away.
Hope for no storm, enough time.
Crush each stem with both hands,

pile the mounded bits chest-high.
Put your heart into it.
Strike steel with flint; make wild sparks

skip like lightning to the gray,
bring sage alive with fire. Pray smoke
curls in swirls so thick it cleanses

even you. Close eyes, breathe deep.
Dream of redemption. As night arrives,
forgive yourself, weep.

>   (published by ***Whatcom Writes Anthology***;
>   republished in **Thick With Conviction**;
>   ***Mapping water***)

Stick horses

Eight-year-old do-gooders,
we rode together on wooden molding

dad hadn't nailed to the wall —
spirited knotty-pine Appaloosas

snaking through trails of flowerbed,
garden, lawn. Leather shoelaces

as reins, toy pistols strapped on,
red bandanas around our necks,

we never got bucked off,
patrolled weed-covered lots,

caught bandits in thickets, jailed them
in the shed just before we were sent

to bed. I cried all night when my pony
became baseboard in the den.

> (published by **Cirque**; republished
> by **Thick With Conviction**)

Tweet from the third pew

Kneeling now
head bowed

seems to pray
hand making cross

other, low, tapping phone.
Priest's eyes on me

hungry, intense, blue
his thumbs down too.

> (published by **Hobo Pancakes**; different version,
> "Head bowed, tweeting from the third pew,"
> published later in 2013 by **Three Line Poetry**)

Poems 2012

300 streams of memory

I dream about time
and the distance between us,

how age settles like silt
in a Montana stream,

replay wounds of cutthroat
laid side by side for gutting,

out of the wicker creel,
where they gasped in unison,

each hoping to see water again,
feel comforting coolness,

dart down to a pool, deep,
lie healing, until time to feed.

>   (published by **Cirque**; republished
>   in *Bellingham Poems*; **Thick With
>   Conviction**; *Mapping water*)

Airport security

Checked in, on the way back,
mazed, lined, ready to screen,

guard grabs pack, digs deep
for weed, bombs, illegal snacks.

Hum a tune as uniformed dudes,
latex-gloved, red wands alert,

give young blonde a private search.
Feet planted on rubber pads,

legs spread, like waving wheat
she sways golden behind plexiglass.

Arms out, eyes shut tight —
wand glides past ankles, knees,

traces breasts, tummy, hips,
thighs. Guards grin, wands fold,

crumpled pack arrives,
airport security, satisfied.

(published by **Urban Resistance**)

Breathing lesson

Summer night, cabin, fishing stream,
storm coming, candlelight,
again Father's demons rise,
force him back in time —

World War II, Philippines,
Leyte battles, Ormoc, Kilay Ridge,
Japan resolve, sniper stealth,
suicide attacks at night.

I ask for the story I know —
am a patient listener,
echo casualty tolls:
forty thousand rising sons die,

fifteen thousand American sons too.
I also recall Mom's whispered tales —
war over, dad home, shouting scenes,
nightmares, screams.

He closes eyes, begins:
Hate finds a way to day,
brings along a friend in rage.
Details pound down like rain —

another surprise attack rebuffed,
GIs bring two Jap captives in,
undo silence, use cigar tip
to trace noses, eyelashes, eyelids.

They strip off helmets, shirts,
shoes, pants, shorts,
sharpen bamboo sticks,
jab points up Japanese butts,

rip through guts, lungs, into heads,
lift the impaled — chant,
dance, with skewered dead
parade the camp.

Frenzy past, shamed soldiers
remove sticks, rake bloody clumps,
in haste, erase the mess —
before sunup, bury what's left.

I am sick — Dad finds brief peace,
listens to me breathe. *At dawn,
he whispers, the stream, the fish —
we'll catch them, then release.*

    (earlier version published
      by **The Curious Record**)

Choosing a nickname for Jesus

We believed it a pious thing
to do. Began with middle initials —
no one knew his full name,
or if the middle actually began with *H*.

A few said *G* for God was nice.
Believers lobbied dutifully
for *Savior*, but the vote went
against them. Logic says don't name

a meat cutter, *Meat Cutter*.
Butcher, maybe, then only for a laugh.
Cross got some votes, died
a lingering death — lack of taste.

Those who questioned *H*
dismissed *Junior* — asked why
it wasn't *God Junior*
in the beginning. And on it went.

Lord, too British. *Messiah*, archaic.
J.C., corporate. *Prince* or *Magic*,
too secular, already used. Consensus
would not arrive. Desperate,

we put the task aside, chose another,
one to worship — nickname Father Time.
Clock Watcher raised our spirits.
Bum Ticker got us high.

    (earlier version published by
    Electric Windmill Press)

Choppy water

Impulsive trip to suture life,
you seek Fishtown, Seventies art colony,
decade-long experiment in bog,
cattail-squatting by painters, poets,
everybody high in marsh-bound shacks,

inspiration delivered twice a day
by Puget Sound tide. Hitch from I-5,
slump colorless in a truck of tulips,
hop down outside this quaint town.
It's been a long year of deaths —

relationship, neighbor, friends —
only not yours, not yet.
La Conner may be a good start,
point you toward Fishtown remains,
provide new direction, maybe north

by redemption. You walk past stacked art,
pallets of it casting long shadows
over First Street, Swinomish Channel
and the gray Sound. Two wrong turns
put you face to face with a church

where one Methodist sits cross-legged,
peers across at Tom Robbins' place,
prays in broken English for a sighting,
like you hopes for hope. Her gaze
says you may be saved by chance

if you bring yourself to believe
poetic fever constitutes fine art,
salt water tastes like good river,
eccentricity cortizones the soul.
She invites you in, whispers low

Robbins never took to Fishtown,
ignored its claim — *deliberate simplicity* —
tromped trails there only in sun.
His house here defies the color wheel,
mocks seclusion with plastic palm tree

clacking out front in the breeze.
Twin Jaguars idle in the driveway,
purr dual temptations — beeline it south,
to Seattle, seek soggy culture,
go to a gallery, take in a chic show.

Sun begins to squat on the horizon,
retreat hinting the answer is flight —
leave Robbins, La Conner, behind,
abandon silly Fishtown quests,
let good life etched in gray go.

Find your own way, steal a black boat,
without holes, paddle northwest
in choppy water, make for Hope Island.
You'll sleep without any tonight,
dream it alive at first light.

(published by **Cirque**)

Congratulations on your breast implants

No tongue piercing, tattoo be damned —
impulsive trip, personal gift,
you stand naked to the navel,

nipples sticking out, like lipstick, red,
guinea pig eyes, wild,
bulging with fright. Doctors

with clipboards line up three deep,
jostle like deer at salt lick,
sketch out big breasts,

same as their wives' — perfect oceans,
private tides — saline, not silicone,
proving your choice wise.

Finally the creator, you also puff lips,
make derrière firm, round, high.
Friends praise you, admire your look,

I paint huge murals of redemption,
sometimes regret — suppress any wish
to sail your new chest.

(published by **Urban Resistance**)

Dashboard savior
(with a nod to Pete Steffens)

Just a glimpse — quick flash really,
swishing past next to a hula girl,
grass skirt swirling, gold, green.

Downtown Bellingham street,
Cornwall, road running out
by Assumption Catholic Church,

near that purple place
where all the peaceniks meet.
Wondered briefly if Second Coming

is capitalized — likely, yes,
because it would be important.
In a '69 Camaro, I think,

something you wouldn't drive
to reach a mountain lake.
Anyway, saw him fly by, upright,

hands in prayer, eyes blue, bright,
glued tight to the dashboard,
not about to go anywhere.

> (published by **Mad Swirl**; republished
> in *Bellingham Poems*; *Mapping water*)

Exhalation
(for Mother)

I saw mother take on death,
sink from cancer to emptiness
the way a balloon, tired

of tugging and squeaking,
breathes long sigh out, turns flat
then hollow, gray, concave —

wrinkled rainbow deflated
at end of day. You vanished too,
exhaled from my life

loveless on your way out.
Deep breath over, my heart
sagged under the shriveled sky.

(published by **Mastodon Dentist**)

Expect no rescue from a Cyclops with delicate hand
(apologies to Nietzsche)

Say life has become a hundred compasses
lying under a magnet
attached to a string. The magnet sways
with each faint breeze. Your needles whirl.

Finding the way north
emerges as your primary problem.
You scan each horizon, search
for ice ax, or engineer-turned-surgeon,

wonder if your health plan will cover
an operation to stop the twirling —
precisely — so your path is clear.
But north may not be the way to go,

what with snow, frostbite, no iPad,
real chance of frozen death —
and glaciers may not offset hell's heat.
Plus, with only one eye, could you focus

once all spinning stopped,
resist temptation, the shapely magnet,
her undulation — block out
every siren's song — regain sanity, vision,

bits of hope? In some circles,
it is said, sculpting angels of snow
brings redemption if you don't know
which way to go.

(published by **Shadow Road Quarterly**)

Going south
(with a nod to Rick Popish)

Turns out, the entire universe
is headed that direction.
Some scientist who broke the news
got a prize — as if we didn't know it

all along, given our intimacy
with *fall, slide, decline, gone bad.*
Think of those politicians, bankers —
riffraff who have gone south,

thieves, on the run, with stolen cars,
diamonds in jars, wives, our hearts.
Pointed not east or west, but down,
away from snow — filching sun,

beach, tequila, rum. We are left
to wonder if light coming from behind
has any hope of catching up.
Or, if rogue galaxies racing north,

suddenly, in their lane, a universe,
no chance to alter speed, swerve —
cosmic crash, splat, the middle,
Earth. Any universe going south

has big trouble — likely pursued
by another, jealous universe,
hurling planets, comets, suns,
cursing, firing black-hole guns.

(published by **Electric Windmill Press**)

Hope

I built a tiny cross of birch
on the ocean shore
where she took all her lovers.

Lit a lantern there at dusk,
told myself I could go on
if it still shone at dawn.

It did.
I said a second night
would bring another day.

At sunset, marauders burned
the cross, blew out my lantern,
carried it off.

I felt warm sand
open herself to moonlight.
She moaned softly in the night.

(published by **Mastodon Dentist**)

Invisible

Bouncing past, skirt aswirl, length,
mid-thigh, she looks through me,

gives her smile to a guy behind.
I'm 52, style my hair, shop J Crew,

whiten teeth, text other dudes,
wear ragged shirts, stylish shades,

check my look in windows,
wink, pose, flirt. But, it's futile.

Something in her genes zaps me —
another man too old, vaporized,

gone in fading light. *Babe, I exist!*
She hears a shadow passing by.

    (published by **Still Crazy**)

The leaving

Too fat to hang at White House Ruins,
doing crank, seduced by metaphor,

pondering divorce number two,
God walks out of math proficiency exam

six ounces early – all the while reciting night sky.
This being America, there were patriots present.

    (published by **Convergence**)

Left for dead

We starve
in war,
ration gas, grow victory gardens,
go without sugar, pretend
chicory is real coffee, deny ourselves
chocolate. We hope to survive
lack of hope to draw
any breath at all. We lie silent,
still as deer after a twig snaps,
in grave-like wait for death
to stop its feeding.

We gorge
in peace,
buy an SUV — vote for those
who rape the Gulf, love BP,
dine out every week, expect ease
in some pink retirement home,
plan to keep our teeth. We believe
our children will visit,
share oily broth. We will be still
as geckos on the wall if asked
did we do anything at all.

(published by **Urban Resistance**)

Painting the soul

Artists learn early:
use shadow to create the face,
body too. Make darkened line a thigh —

swooping smudge, a derrière outlined black
against fading sky.
Purple daub ties highlight to shadow,

a grave awaiting its final filling in.
You departed, lithe,
hips curving down an evening path,

finally obscured by oaks cloaked in gray —
loss erasing any hope to paint the soul.
Charcoal turned to black,

no touch of red, hint of light —
gone, my futile watercolored try
to bring what's dead to life.

    (published by **Cirque**)

Pee hate

I sleep cold at low tide,
back to a naked beach

opening herself to the Pacific.
I own no Nook, cell phone, boat,

wear old jeans, rag coat,
sift trash, eat moldy cheese,

ketchup packs from burger sacks,
fallen fruit off condo trees.

I text my name in water, on sand,
under a moonless sky, pee hate

through the graveyard gate
when headstones tug at my thighs.

    (published by **Bat Terrier**;
     republished by **Carcinogenic Poetry**)

Plotting romance

Fresh out of charm, ambush love —
use the element of surprise

to foster her affection. Hide behind
maroon curtains, step out

with gifts — fish gills, folded,
black widow tequila, elfers on ice.

Or, text a prize — dogsled trek,
remote hot springs, camping overnight,

with you, alone, chance to unwind.
Send photos of scorpions mating —

subtle proof males suffer, bleed, die.
Keep it pure — no games, no lies.

Never permit her a long look
into your molten red eyes.

    (published by **Kumquat Poety Challenge**)

Red sky at night

I carry sea shells three at a time
to safety across beach sprinkled

with fragments of their kind.
Some purple. A few pink.

Beyond reach, evening surf
swirls more than I can rescue

into a rainbow of shards, grinds
perfectly shaped scallops, whelks,

even hawk-wing conchs fine,
then tosses them ashore

to join sand lying white in death
beside yesterday's salt.

You wade, oblivious. My footprints
pool in high tide.

I see wounds, not delight,
slicing red across the sky.

    (published by **Mad Swirl**)

Reprise for hope

"And he drew forth from her breath the stars."
— Leslie Marmon Silko
in ***Ceremony***

I summon a melody from memory,
fear I might not recapture it,
instead, find myself alone,
paralyzed, beached, salty,

unable to imagine you — humming softly —
above me — rocking.
Did we remain that way all night,
incoming tide an accompaniment

outlining us in brine, swirling in time
to our duet, black on white sand,
shadows in motion?
We harmonized until dawn — voices

finally gone, created a ceremony, reprise,
together brought hope alive.
It seemed so easy then —
to sing, to love, to breathe.

>(published in ***Tribute to Orpheus II***;
republished in ***Mapping water***)

Rescue mission

December morning inside my window
I catch orange reflection — ladybugs

piled on more ladybugs, all asleep.
I study markings — black circles

darkened by frost — think I see
what causes them to clump like this.

They must know group warmth
means survival and, so, will starve

all winter — shudder collectively
as snow mounds high outside.

Glass shuts out a bit of cold,
brightens hope, permits belief

they might endure. I tug one loose,
scoop her to a houseplant leaf,

return, rescue more — finally breathe.
At sundown, only tiny shadows freeze.

> (published by **Whatcom Magazine**;
> republished in ***Bellingham Poems***)

SWAG
(with a nod to Lynn Rosen)

It isn't *stuff we ain't getting*,
like rich, or a Lexus —

or no more stinking war.
Or redemption. Folks born pure,

not being sufficiently fecal,
often confuse the end of receiving

with the receiving end.
They have solid faith in tomorrow

always being Christmas,
their birthday, big lottery win —

anyway the day some gaga gift,
wonderful, shining, already given

to politicians, generals, the elite,
most certainly is headed for them —

like silver spit wads to a velvet ceiling,
golden lint to their best wool sweater.

Clearly they dream too much,
don't feel hopeless enough,

need to spend more time
waiting for the really deep stuff.

(published by **Urban Resistance**)

Too fat to hang

The relationship must die.
His thighs have become pillows
wallowing in brie,

hips, strudeled reminders
of Vesuvius choked
not with dust, but cream.

No way to fake it,
breathe deep before nightfall,
ease yourself from underneath

a beefy day, slip off, freshen up,
later creep back lithely, ready
to be on top, talk communication,

quell unease clinging like chunks
of tallow to your soul.
Support groups gone,

friendships growing mold,
vow now to lick back
with hunger, face this foe

head on, swan dive
into hollandaise, swallow hard,
then hold. It's the end —

no good to pretend
nooses are chocolate, gallows
have dessert bars, not stairs.

(published by **Convergence**)

Two dogs, one stick

Patriot, neck red, lake blue, beer, chips,
two pit bulls, a single stick.

Toss it far out, dogs splash in,
furious swim, each grab an end,

yank, growl, turn, churn home.
Their likely treat — one chicken bone.

On the lake,
white wake of foam.

(published by **The Curious Record**)

Unknown clichés
(with a nod to Alex Vouri)

Page filled with blurred words,
I recall vibrant lines, try to forget
each bright place promised,

where death peers over a landscape
of still lifes frozen in primary colors.
I imagine a Yaqui warrior —

not with flute, haunting melodies
moaning through Western movies —
but one who warns old age lays

the final ambush and vanishes,
hinting it may not be enough
to spear setting sun to a place

low in the sky, let it bleed
into dusk, limp by half-light
up a steep draw, or down —

path there less about journey,
more, about redemption,
and forgiveness, which is said

to clear the way. Suns, deer,
stick men with bows, repeated
in paint on canyon walls,

faded reds, golds, greens,
live on, motifs, revered,
not unknown clichés who claim

half-respect only because
they have not yet died.
I rise early each last day,

sit alone, retell my stories,
eyes open, hope dawn bleeds,
remember, try not to sleep.

    (published by **Carnival**)

Verbal agreement

To be, to see,
time of missed connection,
your arriving too late
to join me — on purpose —
drifting off to sleep, reading
to drowsiness, awakening,
finding you turned away,
reaching to click off your light,
tracing your hips, fingers tempted

to stray, but desire brushed aside.
Dreams not inclined to unite,
tomorrow's departure knotted solid
in your sleep, in my chest. Tonight,
late autumn turns to winter,
snow geese flee frozen pond,
wings white, locked in vee,
frost settles thick on love
not to be.

    (published by **The Curious Record**)

Water birthing

I.
We camp at Snake River,
ice crusted on the Tetons,
canoe, peak of our tent.
Fire out, we wait in dim light,
newly together, for the thaw.

You hope I make it come.
I believe your heat
provides necessary melt.
It's a ways, winding, to the end.
At dusk, I call you my moist savior,

worship at your knees,
beg you to bend, absolve me.
All night you try.
We are both half right,
only predicted a beginning,

canoe dropped in swift current
swirling along — hopeful journey
down to Jackson Lake,
Buhl, Ontario,
Clarkston, Pasco, the sea.

II.
We wake to spring snow
heavy as Wyoming saloon dancers,
wet like fresh pain. I stand behind you,
wrap arms like morning glory
around your shoulders, your breasts.

A red blanket drapes us
against the flakes. Rainbow rise groggy
for flies. Jays glide gray sky,
take long drinks from the Snake
deep enough for water birthing.

They squawk for bread, salvation,
life for their young. We are safe,
together, for now canoe upright,
old lovers cleansed from mind.
Snow changes to rain, soaks us,

helps bring a new day. We wait,
you pressed back against me.
Our shadow creeps to moss,
to the river, in mist. Still,
behind you, I drink in all this.

    (published by **Windfall**;
     republished in *Mapping water*)

Poems 2011

Accidental dawn

I fall asleep in some old barn,
drift away on heaps of straw.

A lone rooster awakens me,
crows, *rise, open eyes*.

It is curious how things,
like cocks, can be so familiar:

combs red, feathers shine,
eyes beady, yet intent.

Settled back in golden nest,
I urge the rooster to complete

its song — join in, sing along,
face another accidental dawn.

(published by **Farthermost Dream**)

Aftermath

Sheer unluck let her father find her —
search a snowy road, follow tracks
gone faint beneath powder piling deep,

pine branches suffocating under the load.
Father tramped alone. It was a hunch
to look there, wooded hideout,

daughter's secret place for pondering,
a cul de sac scooped by moonlight
out of frozen night. The car still moaned,

fed fumes to a hose
snaking to the driver's side.
The hose exchanged warmth for death.

It was a night all stars spun away,
when nobody breathed right:
father gasping at the discovery,

daughter still in darkened light,
mother at home, breathless too,
rocking vigil gone quiet.

The aftermath: no future, no hope to sleep,
eyes closed, throats dry,
screams muffled in the night.

(published by **Labyrinth**)

Anemic epiphany

Swirls above tinged gold,
whirl red, purple, green,
color it obvious to Dali, high again,

Perpignan's train station must be
center to the universe —
as if all epiphanies were equal.

In truth some are epiphysis,
spur of dense tissue separated
from mother bone by cartilage,

destined to spend time close,
not attached, alone.
Or, epiphyte, undiscovered orchid

living entire life in crook of tree,
given one small hollow to grow,
denied other source of food,

left in solitude to bloom.
So tromp gloomy mountain paths,
step fast past puddles,

dodge silver rain, examine clouds
for soggy insight, sudden revelation,
rainbowed flash of light,

unbearable, art lost, unseen,
you, epiphytic, on the trail
of anemic epiphanies.

(published by **The Meadowland Review**)

At the Aryan Nations cross burning
(with a nod to Matthew Campbell)

"When they broke open her chest,
her esophagus was so full of holes.
Finally in one bower under her diaphragm
they found a nest of young rats."
                — Gottfried Benn
                      in "Beautiful youth"

You called it a lighting,
said white sparks jumping against night sky
would one day ignite a Christian pyre so fierce

all those on Earth catch fire
except for the believers —
who happen not to be black.

Part of a great design —
and those around me, not reporters
who slipped in, amened and amened

as the children tore in circles around the blaze,
shouted, *devil slaves, burn in hell,*
begged blonde moms

for marshmallows and sharpened sticks.
At dawn I smelled charred sugar
hanging in the Idaho breeze.

    (earlier version published by
    Poetrymagazine.com; different version,
    "At the White Supremacist Cross Burning,"
    published later in 2011 by **Heavy Hands Ink**)

At the Kootenai High School homecoming

Lines of hay bales point the way
to gridiron brown on green,
October sky blue, homecoming game —

fifty students, two cheerleaders, eight players,
yes, even an Idahomecoming queen.
Every farmer turns out, stands amazed

as you gather footballs in, create
a scoring harvest, touchdowns piled
higher on this meadow than anyone

can recall. Even when trees here stood tall,
fought fathers' fathers efforts to break sod,
no story matches memories you plant.

Twenty harvests from now, football seasons
a blur, boys still trying to reap victories,
farmers scratching out a living will retell

this tale — gangly senior rookie receiver,
running over defenders again, again like rows
of mown hay, seven scores, eight, then nine.

But they won't recall your father, wild dancer
across the meadow shouting love to Idaho sky,
won't recount tears welling up his eyes.

(published by **Burnt Bridge**)

At White House Ruins

I hike into Canyon de Chelly,
dream of Pueblo Bonito, place beyond
the horizon, find pictographs —

blue duck, white duck, green feathers,
red heads, gold beaks. They wait to swim
should Chinle Wash flow wide again.

Etched in sandstone cliffs,
the drawings sleep beneath jimsonweed,
salt cedar, Russian olive trees. I wish

for wind to change direction, breathe down
the canyon, with hope. The old Navajo
herding goats by the dry stream

says it happens every thousand moons —
with luck, maybe today. Below ruins
reflected dark in afternoon sun,

only she sees Kokopelli dance past,
golden flute raised in slanted light.
The real ruin is my life. No sacred ducks

swim back and I cannot conjure
ancient ones powerful enough
to erase my soul. Streams of sand

will never flow east to Santa Clara Pueblo,
where, rumor says, hope vibrates within you
and pottery is blacker than black.

(published by **Poetrymagazine.com**;
republished in ***Mapping water***)

Bain Marie

You called it Mary's Bath, dessert,
baptism of alabaster flan — a forgiveness

of sorts — concocted by your black hands.
We watched you skim white coating off milk

brought almost to boil, add lemon, secret sweets,
then fled the room and giggled as you nested

three frothed cups in a glass baking dish.
You winked, poured hot water over a spoon

set on dish bottom so sudden heat did not crack
the glass, filled it half way, then lifted the dish —

slow, slow, no water slosh on hands or flan —
bent low, slid bathers into oven, closed door.

We three nannied, all white, hissed in delight
when the gas burner clicked on.

    (published by **Blinking Cursor**)

Brush with godliness

Outback. Walkabout. So far out
Aborigines and I share hope —
enough water in one day. No more

thirst. No throat cracked like desert clay.
Enough to bathe, to lie back
in water so deep we can drift away,
dream before we wake. Until then,

heat blocks sweat, clogs skin with salty dust,
blisters any tongue daring to whisper
words like *drink*. Or *rain*. We scan

vacant horizon, finally give in, wish
for a funnel cloud of flies.
They come willingly. We bow before them
as they swarm us, blue wings buzzing

in sticky sun. We stand silent,
dream of waterfalls — all the while
caressed by these imbibers of crusted dirt.

They creep into our noses. We breathe them
as they wash us. But mostly we dream
this is our brush with godliness —
until another swarm licks us clean.

(published by **The Curious Record**)

Can you kill a priest with a 1-iron if you keep your head down?

Some poets won't believe,
choose lives not lived from day
to day. Shame has something
to do with it. Maybe out of the blue
a jumbo-jet. A tall building. And all

that blood. Paper's headline reads,
Poet charged with priest's murder
or *Priest found beheaded near St. Pete's*.
No matter. The father's gone — lost —
shoved from plane, pushed off

building, tossed into flames,
hacked to death while praying. And all
that blood. Fate has something to do
with it. The poet may golf. Parishioners,

meekaholics en masse, saw him
behind his church — hitting irons mostly,
slicing balls into graves
across the street. Thought it normal,

said he had a natural swing.
Suddenly this homicide thing.
And all that blood as no choir sings.
Faith has something to do with it.

    (published by **Candidum**)

Count ravens

Together, we maneuver a steep hill
then a loop. I drop you off,

head three streets down,
turn into a cul de sac, mine,

crawl up the walk, through door,
go blind, die. Later, I count ravens

mourning out back. They form
a long line over my grave, caw out

in unison, weep. I kneel, pray,
rise, drive away, intent.

We tend to make death
more important than it really is.

    (published by **Farthermost Dream**)

Dark migration

Pants slung low, belt cinched noose tight,
teeth clenched, handle bars gripped,

another autumn has arrived —
hint of snow, leaves dying, some dead —

time to heed instincts, leave the city.
Alone, no link up, no vee, flee south,

fly past Brooklyn, Jersey, D.C.,
annual effort to shake off dread.

Eyes closed, ride top speed,
stop at green lights, go on the red.

(published by **Everyday Other Things**)

Day of beckoning

Love tends to circle us —
a soaring osprey poised to strike
even though we don't expect to die

of bliss, let alone be eaten.
Like a summer storm, it can blow in,

rock us, knock us, knot our stomach,
nonchalantly lodge romantic grit
in our throat as it makes joy

an indelible part of life. Worrying
that loneliness may be about to end

is of little use — yet we must be watchful.
The constant threat of happiness
sways over us like a translucent noose.

>   (published by **Kumquat Poetry Challenge**;
>   republished in ***Mapping water***)

Doing nothing wrong and still losing
(for Lois and Jim Welch)

You leave, like father departed,
floating off paralyzed,
carried away by a bevy of good men,

me five at the time,
back joyful from bending down
a young pear tree,

fruit not yet ready,
certainly not safe from my raid
on its coming ripeness.

My hands busy in the leaves,
I watched him wave,
paw wild at me, at dying sky.

I dream a bear, poet's orchard,
ignoring Missoula's wrath
to rake in fruit it smelled,

regardless of Blackfeet claim
on land, prayers offered,
ceremonies of hope. Apples

left on trees had no reason to fear,
expected to be spared.
I didn't know emptiness then,

tender-skinned Bartletts,
more vulnerable to bears
and me — permitting sweetness

to waft skyward, be caught
by wind, not cloaked by skin
so thick black bears,

noses lifted, missed the scent,
left too, rumbled off,
intent on Native fruit again.

> (earlier version published by **Cirque**)

Gravity of the situation

Low tide, bright day, late June,
I recline in shade, eyes closed.

Two cats flank me, white one
feigning sleep at my feet —

farther off, le chat noir, on guard,
ears back, listening to us breathe.

I am attuned to my lover, inside,
sighing, rolling out dough

across her sun-streaked stone.
Dusk will arrive after a time.

> (published by **The Curious Record**;
> republished in ***Mapping water***)

Ice caving

Rainier snow blows in low,
collapses crackling in fire.

Twigs, blackened, snap,
become broken arrows of frost,

quivering in cold. They lie pale,
still, hope sparks drift

toward the shared quilt.
He dreams a frantic snowbird

beaks ice. Not once,
but twice. The wind rises,

again unties night,
ropes them together.

They pelt mountain snow
with high-strung fury.

> (earlier version published
> by **Farthermost Dream**)

I eat bitter hearts

Another night plummets on me
from dim stars, like black rope

intent on becoming fat nooses
for hanging good memories of lovers

I've roasted black over an open fire.
Flames dance naked, burn the nooses.

I am moved to stir my artichoke soup
before it becomes so bitter

I cannot eat. What if, in daylight,
life were soup? Would I reach for it

off the high shelf, not care
about price, or pick the store brand,

low down, grab a few cheap saltines
to rub in wounds inflicted

by all the oncoming happiness
and certainty of hunger gone?

I bank my dying fire, lie back,
use a fork to prolong the meal,

slurp away in empty darkness.
I eat bitter hearts last.

(published by **thenumberfive**)

Imposing intelligence

I use double psychology on my cat,
acting as if I am locking her out
so she will dart in.
She cannot miss my line
of dead rats on the porch.

> (published by **Mad Swirl**)

In my dream

we stand together,
naked, on our bed.
The fire licks red.
I reach around, make you

excited. We bounce upward
together, heads slap ceiling
until mattress and frame break.
I reach out, grab the headboard,

try to steady us
so we can stay together.
You push the wood stove over,
it falls into pieces, no coals glow.

I throw one fire brick
at the lamp, break its glass.
Shade still on, it lands upright.
The yellow bulb burns bright.

> (published by **Farthermost Dream**)

Knives in ice

Inuits bury them, handles down,
blades up, add water,

let each freeze solid,
daub the tips with blood.

Lust lopes in before dawn —
wolves believe they've found

seals asleep, streams full of salmon,
caribou laid out end to end.

They lap up the offering,
ignore it is their own blood

they drink to fullness,
to weakness, to sleep.

Curled frozen on red ice,
frosted furs offer Inuits hope,

life with color, warmth at night.
Arctic wind retains howling rights.

(published by **Mad Swirl**)

Late call from Plato's cave

Father, I say we're not chained in.
Hope grows here like mushrooms.
No shackles chafe, our eyes

don't blur red. Shadows
and cavern walls show no signs of hate.
Greeks called these sights illusions.

We've heard it before. Stories of sky,
sun above — only babbling,
not truth we can chisel our initials in.

Proof comes daily like refried air.
Screens stretch silver, stalagmite
to tite, ninety channels of beaches,

blondes glowing in the sun,
surviving crime at night.
Tell those who peddle some other life

the votes are in. Only cop and doctor shows
were elected. Walls they call fake
we call walls full of drama,

making distant quakes, wars, coups
so vivid even assassinated dictators
live again, parade-proud, their tanks

triumphant on the six o'clock news.
Yes, Dad, forget tales of mountains, trees,
ocean breeze. We refuse your stance

even if you dissect an entire TV station,
hold out bloody tumors as evidence
in your living-color hands.

   (published by **Blinking Cursor**)

Missed connections

Diving gull,
crust of bread you tossed.

Sudden swerve,
passing truck. No escape

with both life
and bread intact.

I found her in high grass
hurling herself at the sky

with one good wing,
gave her healing box

covered up with dampened cloth,
set her aside to mend.

A second gull circled for days.
You only said

All the bread is gone.

   (published by **Mastodon Dentist**)

Montana chicken-killing day

Big sky full of sky, early dawn,
sharp ax near chicken shed,
cocks awaken Dad

but crow no warning
of April death. Young pullets
step high, clench yellow feet,

combs poised in early breeze.
They peck an uncertain pattern,
send up collective cluck as I shoo them

toward the chopping block.
Jobs pre-assigned — Dad, ax,
Mom, canvas apron, gutting knife,

Sister, scalding tub,
dunk limp birds, feathers red —
also condemned to pluck the dead.

Grandma, tend alcohol flame,
singe pinfeathers, scorch skin
before Mom's emptying begins.

My job, grasp victim,
head on block, secured by stick,
gold-eyed stare deflected a bit —

Dad's swift chop, head gone,
neck not pinned, free
to spray wet grass red.

Decades past, white breasts,
thighs plastic-wrapped —
memories, childhood screams,

Montana dreams, chickens,
me, on the run, zigzag dizzy,
not squirting blood toward the sun.

(published by **Windfall**)

No more desert

No more desert, love grows
as you make deep grooves
with your sharp hooves.

    (published by **Three Line Poetry**)

Noose

Joy hovers above us,
a condor poised to strike

when we are not ready
to die of bliss, let alone

be eaten. It shadows us
for months, goes without water,

catches us still dour,
sucking on belief in no love,

praying for a life of hopelessness,
bits of cynical grit clogging throats.

We think our loneliness will last,
believe it possible to feed

at the trough of depression forever —
but we must be on guard.

Happiness sways over us
like a hangman's noose.

    (published by **Candidum**)

Painting lesson

Onyx spider drawn to spin
from frond on fern to fence,
and back again, lost control

as I thrashed by, let silk out fast,
spiraled wide, around, splashed down
near brush dipped deep

in white paint tin. My ruthless youth,
Genghis Tim to arachnid kin
dunked like this — some forced to swim,

others stroked latex on window trim —
this time, I grabbed a twig,
dipped it in, scooped coated spider

to cupped palm of withered hand.
Garden hose set on drip, I rinsed
her whiteness black again.

>(published by **Sue Boynton Poetry Contest**; republished in *Poetry Walk: The Second Five Years*; *Mapping water*)

Picture please

She goes, *like if you don't mind*
so I go, *I would be happy to,*

and dip deep, stir the very bottom,
aware of pleasure I am about to serve,

and as I slowly draw up,
I go, *are you sure you want*

even more, she goes, *yes,*
yes, sir, like Oliver, more,

I go, *then, for you, happiness,*
this huge cup of soup. I pour.

(published by **Everyday Other Things**)

Poem to name perfume after

He could have awakened dead
but didn't — instead, clipped her poems,
stories, carried them crumpled,

reread each over tea,
hung her picture beside Van Gogh's,
then moved it to Matisse.

He tried to catch glimpses
in flushed daze,
her rushing for a train,

swinging in the park,
closing nighttime blinds,
pelted down by rain —

once, eased close behind
in crowd, breathed deep,
inhaled her scent,

touched sleeve by accident —
in sideways glance, hoped to see
her eyes change, gray

to green. He believed each day a test —
name perfume lingering when she left.
Obsession.

(published by **Thick With Conviction**)

Poem to scrape pelts by

Mixed memories of father, mink,
high school crush on Brie.
I should have known decades later
Lycra look-alikes passing by
would bring her to mind

so fine at thirty-five
I'd wash bedding six times a week,
hang sheets out each day
rather than let her memory fade.
Word had it she was great in bed,

as fine as mink, or so
the saying went. Who really knew
mink screwed so well,
if they walked Brie's road,
spent summer nights

outside picket fence, wished
for glimpse, her shape on shade,
lusty memory for the coming days.
In truth, caged mink gave up life
in poison fumes as Dad slid stone

to skinning knife. He denied them sex,
stripped skins white as Brie's shade,
pelts soon tacked to tanning slates.
They dried flat in lines,
formed nightmares, dreams

for me to own — Dad, Brie, mink,
jumbled together — not alone —
pencil on paper, sullen poem.
Not skinning knife,
not sharpening stone.

(published by **Candidum**)

Post-cuckold stress syndrome

I wake wet, slick,
throat clogged, try to breathe,
renew effort to escape nightmares,
you choking me again.
I wish sleep back —

life lived in reverse,
caramel Jesus smiling, our pleasure —
believe two hours will suffice
but face unholy flashbacks
until dawn lays down

a new layer of salted dew.
I pray for more.
Hail today — or snow.
Something not painful.
Tales with happy endings

told by a savior. Just no repeat,
no shower together,
no fake love in dark,
you on top of me,
of him later.

I watch and drown,
dragged down by these replays
ripping me awake
to dampness and hope
I find a strong rope today.

(published by **Heavy Hands Ink**)

Primary love, complementary colors

End of day, I cook with you.
Sunset, orange — sky fades gray
from blue. We light candles,

mostly red. Flames turn green
at night's black edge.
An oval moon rises yellow-gold,

gives clouds beneath a purple hue.
We lie entwined, two chefs, hot food —
famished lovers, cordon bleu.

    (published by **Bellingham Herald**)

Publishing in The New Yorker

Manhattan black, laptop tipped back,
whiskey fifth too, dim the lights,
summon your muse.

Recall New England, streams flaccid,
leaves in decay,
you up from the city,

lover cast away, your ongoing curse —
brilliance, wit, rage.
Reflect on drugs, depression,

suicide tries, abuse at home,
prison-camp torture,
suffering alone.

Friends come, go — all, shallow,
obtuse, vain — none seeing truth,
the midnight again. So, unbutton

lithe images, make metaphors moan.
Somehow pour out
another self-obsessed poem.

    (published by **Candidum**)

Rafting with Fitzgerald
(with a nod to Dan Breeden,
Tom Husby, and Steve Fitzgerald)

You recall that trip — Idaho,
rapids, righteous Salmon River,
three boats, twelve of us, and Fitz?

Bodacious bounce at low water,
Zelda dancing in panties,
kicking high below the falls,
tempting most of us, jump in,

jump in? You were there —
downed all our whiskey in two nights,
feared we'd die of thirst.

Remember, day six— salvation —
we floated by a raft of diabetics,
Fitz walked across the water,
traded diet soda pop for beer.

    (published by **Candidum**)

Sponges

How can we —
home, garden, shade,
morning after rain,
chives, thyme, grapes,
black cat at our feet –
soak in all this peace?

    (published by **NitTwitts: A Collection
    of Twitter-Length Poems**)

Too much hope

Waves always waist-high,
fifty miles of white beach,

sun never clouded, Dylan on CD.
Model's body for you, big pecs for me,

teeter-totter perfectly balanced,
no teet, no tot,

Odysseus without Cyclops,
Sisyphus on top. Climaxing for hours,

sad tears never dropped,
love always beginning,

mate faithful each night,
death not coming until 105.

We'll have skylights in our coffins,
designer sunglasses for dead eyes.

    (published by **The Curious Record**)

Trek

Fingers trace smooth grooves,
furrows between your ribs,

from backbone near spine —
guide meridian of the soul —

to front. The path is steady,
slow. Each slopes south,

rounds your side, points toward
the desert, abdomen,

brown, flat — and beyond.
I know I should climb ridges,

cross one valley, then another,
head north to explore,

meld minds, blurt out ideas,
say something profound.

But, magnetic south
draws me down.

    (published by **Farthermost Dream**)

Use two pillows, sleep fast
(with a nod to Alex Vouri)

Dreams swirl in like snow,
drift in piles — lovers, loved.
I wrap each in burlap,

lash openings against the cold.
Some vanish by dawn —
frozen, quiet, quick to go.

Others — warmed, stroked,
unbind themselves — return, hot,
mute my muffled screams.

Candles I disrobe you by
drip waxy fire, memories wafting
across each fold and pleat.

Slow to know love from heat,
I warm myself in steam
rising from the open seams.

    (published by **Mad Swirl**)

Web mutiny

These flat screens tie off dreams,
pirate eyes while pixeled derrières

float by, round ghosts awash
in curvy seas of slender light.

Nightmares should wake us,
promise morning, hope, rum in vats,

not more bottoms bobbing past.
To break free, we must mutiny,

seize Web Mistress, take control,
gauge wind, starboard tack —

then, bound for home, torture night,
use her thong to cleat hitch dawn.

We will expect no thanks
as she sways to the plank.

(published by **Farthermost Dream**)

Poems 2010

All quiet on the Iraqi front

TV reporters, embedded, blurt praise
of heroes, ours, with guns, run tape
not showing blood-bought freedom,
democracy, oil — mostly oil.

Smoke and soot, both black,
roll across the plain.
A snake, charcoal vined,
slides in search of any green,

S-path drifted over by grime.
Not to be outdone, daffodils
poke through blackened earth,
sway briefly, see blooms die

half-yellow, half-hearted.
Children flirt with hope,
ignore extra layers of dirt,
play tag in willow grove, boughs

bent and broke. Parents rock
on mud-brick porch, recall rumors
of war not waged, bombs not dropped,
future not gray.

They try to remember how
a normal day presents itself: blue sky,
dipping sun, clouds hinting rain.
Again, tonight's storm

will form puddles of red —
at dawn, another search
for handprints, child-size,
although the hands are gone.

    (published by **Apathy is Easy**)

Bats at the hummingbird feeder
(with a nod to Penny Brown)

Fast, greedy, known to swoop in,
sneak drinks from hummingbird feeders,
wings all the while flapping.
You know — like politicians.
I read it somewhere, but also hear
their flutter on summer nights.

Bats must not be allowed to drink
all the nectar. Hummers need it
to keep them going: Rufus, white spots
on tail; Annas, similar to Allens,
heads, violet, females, green.
They're on the wing somewhere,

  probably for food. In winter they fight over
  remaining bugs. Bats look on,
  ask winners for their vote. Sad. Look it up
  on Wikipedia. And, change nectar every week
  so hummers don't get rabies
  creeping up their slender beaks.

    (published by **The Curious Record**)

Chicken
(found poem, Town Tavern bathroom,
 Port Townsend, Wash.)

Just when I thought
it couldn't get any better

she brought out the chicken
and, boy,

could she serve
chicken.

> (published by **Caper Literary Journal**;
> republished by **Bellingham Herald**)

Deserted advice

Believe — now is the best time
to hope. Forget loneliness. Suspend
all gathering doubt, bind your wounds.

Embrace change in its run to shore.
At dusk, gaze into a tidepool.
Find the resolve to search for purple.

Give yourself your word. Kindle seaweed
on the beach at midnight. Without warning,
send this note in a bottle to your lover.

> (published by **Kumquat Poetry Challenge**;
> republished by **Thick With Conviction**;
> *Mapping water*)

Editing your life

Today's chore — weed the photo album,
purge snaps with hints of ragged times,
condense images of all those years
with husband number five. If pressed,

recall his name and flaws, not his eyes.
Perhaps another marriage,
you once again a blushing bride.
Or a child given up at birth

has found you, wants to see your past,
know the mom she missed — your tiny lie.
Or simply, a life with him you want to forget.
Toss out snapshots — forest hikes,

hot spring nude romp in mist, campfires,
tents, untangling fishing lines. Throw
wedding photos — vows, kiss, cutting cake,
honeymoon escape. Excise wrapping

Christmas gifts, family trips, your children
asleep in his arms. Keep one photo, New Year,
him in back among siblings posed,
smiling faces, crooked rows.

    (earlier version published by **Labyrinth**)

Eternal life

Scientists, lacking hobbies, family, wives,
have found molecules

making up our bodies
to be four billion years old.

The good news from this:
we have eternal life.

The bad news is
we've been drift nets, oil spills, coffin lids.

   (published by **Poets for Living Waters**)

Fencing in darkness

To begin, make a list. One, sword,
pointed, thin. Two, mask
with mesh, dark, tight. Three,
wire, barbed strands twisted sharp.
Four, a counselor or priest,
confessor, friend. Someone
to deal with tears, sins,

lift spirits up again.
Five, light, probing, bright,
letting nothing hide.
To stay alive, survive,
make backup plans of plans.
Then re-read Frost, Jung,

recite "Mending Wall" by moon
or sun. Know what
must die, let live again.
Learn to feign, sway,
drive point in, first at dusk,

then in day. Practice blindfolded,
eyes shut. Dream at night,
knees curled to chin.
Shun mirrors, learn to fence well,

others out, yourself in.
Know enough to suffocate
before dueling death again.

    (published by **13 Miles from Cleveland**)

Fragile X parent
(with a nod to Chuck Luckmann)

Again he paces at our bed, restless,
but happy as eighteen previous years,
now six feet tall, at six a.m. —

he needs a shave, his diaper, full.
He roams her side, then mine,
gives the comforter a tug.

Today, dentist. Dentist, he says.
Today. Dentist. Dentist.
We had been seizing pre-dawn quiet,

hoping again, just sex,
the two of us, alone,
but Clonidine worn off, he is early,

not understanding chromosome weakened,
passed down mother to son — hope diluted —
instead, intent on the dentist,

and, yes — *clean me, wipe,*
cereal in the deep bowl, white,
not the blue, the white.

Like yesterday, and the day before,
he will wear the black pants, blue shirt
with stripes, watch the same cartoons,

eat Special K again, not fully know
custody, ward of state, guardian,
emancipation, judge, group home —

only care she or I awake, rise,
turn on Scooby Doo, find clean diapers,
fill the deep bowl, pure white.

> (published by **Convergence**)

Gourmet

Radio ads tantalize — catfish nuggets
stuffed with dates, diced imitation

loon fillets, simmered beaver tie-dyed ribs,
deep-fried raccoon, sauteed squid,

Atlantic ranch-raised dolphin cakes,
crusted eel, gecko chunks, malt-ball stuffed

elephant trunk, wine-infused escargot,
albino skunk flown in from Greece,

broasted owl eyes, gorgonzola leeks.
Quite by accident my python exudes

spicy rhino hollandaise cream
on seal-skin seats in my SUV.

> (published by **The Momo Reader**)

Headboard
(with a nod to Malinda Finney Briggs)

Packing mainly blame with me,
I begin my retreat — Canada,

mineral springs, posh resort,
steam rising to melt new snow,

forgiveness cloaked beneath fuzzy robes.
But guards believe I hide much more —

won't hop pool to pool, then cool,
need no massage, instead will wake

wet from dreams, guilty screams,
rip innocent headboard off the bed.

They search my van, my pants
for weed, for crack, for blow,

for hidden gun coaxed to explode
by parted lips just hours ago.

(published by **Heavy Hands Ink**)

The heaped wheelbarrow

So many *depends*
heaped

in your wheelbarrow
stained

autumn-brown, and me,
afraid again,

beside buckets
filled

with golden rain.

    (published by **The Momo Reader**)

If

my late father could open
a small window,
say one that slides,
not even much bigger than phones
teens carry around —

a window not screened
or double-paned — if he would
and could stick out
one hand, toss down
brief note, better yet

press lips to outside,
shout he had planned
to phone the day he died,
let me know finally
he loved me, missed me,

be certain
I was ok,
if he could, it would
give courage, at least enough
to e-mail my son,

tell him I'm sad,
lack excuses for not being
in touch, miss him,
relay bits of news,
say I'm putting in

bigger windows, his old room,
ones that open,
open wide,
confide my heart
has been acting up again.

    (published by **The Tipton Poetry Journal**)

I herded flies, Buzz, when I dyed
(with a nod to Emily Dickinson)

It was lack of color. Poetry without hue.
Like your name before Buzz —
also without cadence — something like Bruce.
Suffice it to say
my cloth was not vivid.

So I turned to black — purple gone bad —
hoped for morning fog,
faint blush in summer sky
providing a bit of tint to life.
Then they arrived, dark cloud, en masse,

normal for flies; they're not geese,
after all. No vee,
no leader, gaggle a distant speck
in their minds, they circled without cease —
buzz repeat and repeat —

inspired something from nothing,
creative irritation, poetry that sings.
That night, still high, without light,
I colored them all violet,
right down to their iambic wings.

 (published by **The Curious Record**)

Ironing my face

Guilt leads on to inferno, hell.
I am feverish, bloated, pale,

think dogs buried bones in my cheeks.
I need immediate redemption

but no Nordic savior can cool
my heart, ice storm my pores,

whisper frozen chants to save me.
Ironing works for sheets, also white,

straightens their bleached lives,
unwrinkles sleeplessness awhile.

Perhaps set the iron on *high*,
use steam around each eye,

crease my lips, chin, nose. Purgatory
should smooth my wadded soul.

 (published by **The Momo Reader**)

John two sixteen

I forgot the first line to this poem —
words probably round, hard, firm.
Drooping, no doubt, it will return,
faith of the Second Coming
being the important thing.
I do recall the poem's main thrust:
somehow convince my son John
he cannot give his god
a multiple-choice exam and then
expect to grade it. Ah, the story.
John believes he can test God
by setting up a predicament
clearly one-sided, so loaded
the Big Guy will be forced
to send a clear sign —
lightning bolt down a choice.

John says put your home for sale,
price it so high only a fool
would buy. Then, if someone
does drive past, turn, swoop in
bearing a satchel of cash,
you'd be rich and God's intent, clear:
John, sell your home, move family
to a cave. But this is not Pascal's Gamble,
four choices based on logic —
instead, a complicated mess
of faith placing God
on the real estate escrow seat.

I forgot the last line
to this poem too; it's probably phallic,
missile headed toward a strike
but returning to its silo site.

    (published by **The Momo Reader**)

Late warning

If my lovely vulture swoops by,
dark wings spread eight feet,
blood caked on gold beak,

last prey, me, old meat,
if she demands your heart,
please sigh, sob, cry,

whine, fret, lie,
sidle toward her after awhile,
kneel, cling to her feet,

beg her to stay until she leaves.
Never, never offer up
your love, red wine, a little brie.

    (published by **Caper Literary Journal**
      & **Luna Luna Magazine**)

Letter found on a flash drive near the B.C. border

Linda, your memory steeps,
gets me up at dawn.
I hang on — Birch Bay, U.S.A.,

far northwest corner
of Washington state. My life
floats in Puget Sound

toward the border. If only you
could save me now.
How did we ever fall out

of touch — your hand, mine
brushing by, 1973? We got on
so well — you with Johnny, me,

all three singing, *Bye bye
Miss American Pie*, hating Nixon,
getting high, loving silent on my boat,

Johnny, drunk, snoring
as our mingled breath
brought moistness to purple slits

of dawn, the dappled sky.
How did such drift not grab and hold?
Please phone, e-mail, risk a note.

Let's sing Brautigan, Lennon,
to life again, drink red wine,
make love all night — this time, moan,

reverse the bloody flow —
determine for ourselves
which way not to go.

   (published by **Cirque**)

Note on my windshield

Apartment complex, lot full of cars,
black Hondas all around mine,
I feared paper under wiper
some neighbor's threat —

no parking on the line.
Here is all your stuff, I think.
Your words have been lies —
poems, notes, cards, everything.

All lies. Also, the inkwell you wanted.
Take care of it, please.
I will always love you
no matter how you treated me.

Good luck. I hope you get
what you want. God's grace
and mercy as well. I tossed
the note, combed lot for sack,

package, taped-shut box,
hoped for pants, belt, stylish hat.
I searched for the inkwell
until darkness fell.

> (published by **The Curious Record**)

Richter Scale

I'd better go – love slides away,
your lover says, letting you know
hers has become 0 point 0,

but yours – trembling, fear,
being abandoned again —
registers over 8 point 8.

You recall first high school lust,
that sudden tremor, how the Ford
shook under moonlight

as she rubbed against you,
bringing meaning to quake.
Rank such love, 2 point 5.

And, marriage, frequent sex, finally,
a decade nesting, not alone,
definitely 4 point 3 —

later point 6, or point 5,
affection capsized. Then,
this major quake, long, rolling love,

sudden, deep, recurring,
at times 9 point 3, now everything
down, serious seismic heartbreak,

no way to rebuild,
rubble the end of mountains,
daylight, seasons, tides —

even chance in the ruin,
entire coasts broken free,
out of sight in a choppy sea.

(published by **The Momo Reader**)

Screw the pretentious poets

Late evening, I was reading
a lame poem in The Sun
and it was getting to me.
Before dusk, before I saw
the dark magazine, before art left,

I had been writing about Exxon
escaping penalty for its spill,
or was it how a lover
who pureed my guts,
by leaving became a metaphor

for consumers, a society in love
with throwing everything away,
people too, or how patriots push zeal
on the rest of us,
how a friend of mine on a raft trip

traded diet sodas to diabetics
for beer when he ran out of whiskey,
how breathing insulation
you're installing in a church attic
is like doing crack, how God

would walk out of a math proficiency exam,
about how to choose a nickname
for Jesus — or how a geek
invited to the Donner Party would eat
his girlfriend last because she was delicious —

or maybe facing cancer decades after
you dismantle nuclear bombs,
certainly about sleep not coming
for a lifetime after you've buried heads
of Japanese soldiers our World War II Army

paid natives two dollars for — and, by the way,
about hope. Anyway, so screw poets who write
of New England, those pastoral places
where they find insight and deep meaning,
not real life below them in the city,

they who run off to the MLA convention
with their tight little couplets.
Screw them as thanks for all poets
who are free enough to write
about what writhes — not about

what some English prof at Columbia
says poetry should be. Screw those poets
and the critics with their Ph.D.s
who haven't really lived, write crap,
boring, pedantic, all about me.

   (published by **Apathy is Easy**)

Slick — to Exxon then and BP now

I.
Number of "23 species seriously depleted by the
1989 Exxon Valdez oil spill that have recovered — 1"
      — Harper's Index, Sept. 1997

"The current worst-case estimate of what's spewing
into the Gulf (of Mexico by BP's Deepwater Horizon
oil well) is 2.5 million gallons a day."
      — AP, June 24, 2010

You brought new meaning to robber baron,
taught us to know black snow on tundra,
scrape frozen sod primed with promises
even Arctic fox knew to be lies.
Your lawyers slapping backs in bars,
buying free drinks — all these brought sadness

even dutiful glaciers couldn't scrub away.
We tromped black sand, piled oily birds,
seals, cheek-high, set them ablaze,
watched the pyre outshine frosty dusk.
Our breath froze white on darkened beach.
That night we burned ice to stay warm.

II.
"This was a tragic and terrible event, and one for
which the company has paid dearly. ..."
      — Exxon lawyerDellinger arguing
       before the U.S. Supreme Court,
       Feb. 2008

The rocky shore lay bare, helicopters,
skimmers, hoses, booms, all gone,

seabird washers, beach workers,
dead sea otters, harbor seals,
even the Valdez, gone too.
No more hot salt spray

spreading the goo around.
A lone mallard struggled in, staggered
up the beach, tried to preen,
gave up, too many green feathers
matted down. He turned, wobbled
to the Sound, where he drowned.

III.

"The U.S. Supreme Court gutted punitive damages awarded to victims of the Exxon Valdez ... from $2.5 billion to $500 million."
— The Seattle Post-Intelligencer
June 26, 2008

"BP CEO Tony Hayward ... took a break from his oil spill duties in the Gulf of Mexico to attend a yacht race ... in the English Channel."
— Politics Daily, June 1, 2010

We buried another fisher today, dropped
a handful of greasy sod, a few black rocks
in the grave — at dusk kindled his boat,
its hold empty twenty-one years
until BP killed the Gulf. We set our tribute
adrift, watched the whole bay catch fire,

flames race to shore, climb sand,
burn a row of skiffs. No terns turned high,

no eagles swooped low. Out on the Sound
another of your tankers droned.
In its wake, nine sleek crows
escorted another bloated walrus home.

   (published by **Poets for Living Waters**;
   accepted by British composer James Wood
   for a composition on the Apocalypse)

**This being America,
there were patriots present**

In the desert
I saw creatures,

warlike, obsessed,
running about with swords,

each cutting open another's head.
Won't you miss

your brains? I asked.
What? they replied,

and skipped off together,
free.

   (published by **The Curious Record**;
   republished by **Poetry Pacific**)

Poems 2000-09

Cellphone dolor at Sea-Tac airport
(with a nod to Theodore Roethke)

I have seen inexorable growth
of cellphones sprouting like beans,
some yellow, others slender, green,

leafed out romaine, almost sweet,
held near mouths,
smelly tongues, decay of gums,

lies blown stale into shiny leaves.
Others, gold, peeled-back corn,
cradled tight by sweaty hands

sowing grime on kerneled rows.
And, black ones, sleek,
like Asian eggplants, curved, petite,

held to waxy ears, shriveled, old.
Too often I have boarded flights
phoneless, carried only hope to stow,

noticed my thumb twitching,
quite alone,
not yet covered by a film of mold.

(published by **Jeopardy**)

Deep end
(with a nod to Jayne Anne Phillips)

Summer, 1960, me thirteen at the time,
high school girls budding out,
lolling poolside, diving in.
I cannot touch bikinis, skin —

only watch them chat, boyfriends
on lunch breaks, fingers chain-linked,
their guys fenced outside.
They lie in lawnchairs, squirm,

lick dilly bars, gossip,
splash on sunscreen,
slather thighs, backs,
sometimes nap.

The blonde I want, tanned by noon,
lets one strap fall loose,
shows off a milky stripe
running its path down. She gives

her steady a cleavage glimpse,
fair trade for snowcone dipped in red,
handed slowly over the mesh.
They all frost white in freckle cream,

bake in afternoon sun.
I try to make out
what they laugh about,
catch brief snatches as they murmur,

heads bent together, orchids drooped
in prayer. They shower, shampoo,
perch on Elvis Presley towels,
twirl plastic curlers tight,

section off each other's hair,
rat-tail combs busy
scurrying on their heads,
promise of Jackie Kennedy look to come.

They writhe on tummies, butts swooping,
legs toasting brown as curlers dry.
I suspect they go all the way,
daydream of it as they play Crazy Eights,

keep score on Black Jack gum wrappers.
In the heat, I swim endless laps,
do underwater somersaults.
I spin furiously in the deep end.

   (published by **My Favorite Bullet**)

Defense for mailing panties back

In hindsight, big mistake,
no doubt. Found in dryer load, slightly damp,
thought them yours after nine-day stay,
scattered clothes about my place.

Bra, thirty-four B, on rocking chair, jeans
crumpled by the stairs, lacy tees
draped on bed. No color mistake or lie,
red or pink, not pure white.

No misunderstanding size,
eight or nine, instead of five.
Not low-rise bikini or tiny thong
baring cheeks, upper thighs. Dirty job,

finding owner — mystery intensified
when people try each other on for size.
To be sure, miscommunication eight
on Richter panty-owner scale.

Sent wadded here again by mail,
I pinned them up at Lost and Found —
near the fabric softener,
I think it's Bounce.

    (published by **Jeopardy**)

Destined to rhyme
(for Carolyn)

I keep our poems together,
carry them with me, stowed
in my pack. Tied by fishing line,
they've grown used to folds
of each other's pages, yours
more worn than mine, from reading,
from being smoothed. Sometimes,
by moonlight, on a whim,
I untether and scatter them,
pick one at random,
savor it awhile,
imagine you close by my side.
After a time,
they swim together naturally,
snuggle into place, dive deep
lie intertwined on the bottom.
I get the impression
they don't mind being bound.

> (earlier version published
> by **Trestle Creek Review**;
> republished by **Bellingham Herald)**

Doing crank

Breathing insulation
I unroll in church attics

is like doing crank.
Three days later

when I come down, I believe
this is how it feels

when people wake up
dead.

>(published by **Sqajet**; different version, "Salvation," published in 2016 by **Aberration Labyrinth**)

Financial planning session

Mountain camping, night sky starred,
crickets chirping, lantern light.
Father clutches four wallets,
each fat with cash, looks back
at seventy years with profit, knows
he must hoard them
but cannot remember why.

I try to help him understand,
do my best to teach.
In all the universe, I say,
*one planet like ours whirls
every two solar systems, or three,
at most a handful per galaxy.
They spin along, crusts cooling*

*like croissants in some galactic oven,
then, for one second —
maybe a million years our time —
the potential for life.
But orbits decay, north stars change,
and they wobble like tired tops
toward snow, ice, night.*

*One beats the odds, creates beings,
intelligent, with dreams.
They perish — hate, war, greed.*
His back to me, Father, still quiet,
feigns sleep. *Tomorrow*,
he finally murmurs, *let's talk
stocks, bonds, annuities.*

(published by **The Curious Record**)

Fresh graves in black sand

I lie beached, still,
prepare to gather hope,
in sun as if death
could not surprise me,
like kelp ashore to dry.

I guard a deep tidepool,
plan at night to save flesh
in bright shells, fling back
those which are purple.
I will give them new life.

No tide can reach me here
or so I believe.
But night surf, without hands,
swirls in effortless,
scoops fresh graves in black sand.

(published by **Bathyspheric Review**)

Hear no evil

Montana campfire. Cabin buried by night.
My father's past carved fifty years
around eyes gone half blind.
Finally he lets slip

one piece of a camouflaged life.
South Pacific, New Guinea,
second world war, Army directive:
Turn Japanese back here,

now, for good, or watch them swarm
Australia's beaches, Rising Sun
matching Coral Sea wave for wave.
There, then, desperate men give war

a new face, obey orders, pay natives
two dollars silver for each enemy head.
Dad, back from regular killing, for rest,
for good, undertakes a new mission.

Bury skulls, some on bamboo stakes,
others piled about the camp.
Carry them sleepy, two at a time, smiling.
Fill trenches-turned-graves. Fling others

into caves with decaying comrades
frozen in battle crouch, licked to death
by flames thrown in like afterthoughts.
Shovels cover memories deep in loam.

GIs, Dad welcome orders — *EARS ONLY* —
this exacts a fresh toll. Husbands
snip orchids listening to moonlight
from dozing children, wives. A generation

will hear no evil, detect no lies.
Dad finds it easy to slip off to sleep.
I drink sake all night, fend off
dreams with a carving knife.

> (earlier version published by **Jeopardy**;
> republished in ***Weathered Pages:***
> ***The Poetry Pole***)

In which the romantic writes
one last poem before having a beer

You've come this far
alone.
No bouts with dancing cat fever, no need
for earrings, nose rings,
tattoos of naked women lolling about,

breasts pointed up your arm.
Only one, discreet — teen, no bra, demure,
finely etched between ankle and knee.
You don't question why she poses half nude.
Think her a student

reduced to modeling, topless
dancing — but not turning tricks.
All for a masters degree,
probably in psychology,
so she can test children

whose parents drink too much.
If those kids memorize the presidents,
Gettysburg Address, win
enough spelling bees, they'll be deluged
with scholarships, go to college.

Become alcohol counselors, latter day
Carrie Nations swinging axes
of sobriety. They'll help drunken parents
realize kids must have
skateboards, designer jeans,

cellphones, call-waiting,
a whole supply of friends
to put on hold.
You cling to belief
most lovers find happiness

with only one mate. Form unions
lasting a lifetime. Continue
to dance, talk, joke,
most certainly share hopes
and hurt well beyond

those first-date kisses filling jeans
with sparks you believe
kindled true love. You are not the first
to have such hope.
You are not the first to drink alone.

    (earlier version published by **Jeopardy**)

My only son
(for John)

Midday heat lets me believe
I see waves retreat
in layers. Water fleeing moist sand
fearful itself of being
stretched flat to dry.

A final shadow on the dampness
conjures up my only son.
He sits brown,
cross-legged at ebb's edge,
humming in heavy mist,

beached shaman offering memories,
forgiveness,
a little salt. I wait breathless,
hope a wave brings another vision.
In its wake I suspect

it shall be him, alive again,
damp, salty,
chanting prayerful over me.
It is only by design
what I believe, I see.

    (published by **Bathyspheric Review**)

No design on the sky

Twenty years too late, I notice
clouds don't have edges
but flow smoothly, beveled,
like you lying close then,

my fingers tracing skin,
lower back to upper thigh,
roundness eager to bend.
Edges. Corners. Even the words

do not yield, instead
bring aggression to life,
lie menacing, fecund with force,
speak ill of humans because little

in nature has a sharp edge.
Granite tips round slightly,
flat sides of leaves curve, merge
with subtlety we ignore.

Leaves do not impose will,
only flutter in harmony,
cloud-like, bowing, curling,
creating roundness, autumnal pose

without resistance, seasons spent
not knowing how to use force.
Clouds have no edges.
They make no design on the sky.

(published by **Sqajet**)

No way in

Something there is
that does not love a window shut.
So I opened mine,
invited in sunlight, cry of gulls,
salty scent of bay,
tide in retreat,

not sloshing rocky shore.
I left it open even during rain,
shivered, clutched tea with both hands,
sought a bit of heat,
wished the whole coast inside —
gulls, salt, sea,
you leaving him for me,

to put down doubt,
bow in concupiscent splendor.
I waited, alone,
watched shadowed sunbolts
spin among clouds, dance past
the half-glassed-in solarium,

refract, bounce back,
make me understand
neither tide nor sun nor you
could ever come completely in.
So, in winter's darkest month,
fingers cold, I latched
my open window closed.

(published by **The Tipton Poetry Journal**)

Pawnshop

Sky gray, out of hope, lover gone,
I take my best sonnet
to Gordon's poem and pawn,
ask for cash, half value
on the open market — still nothing
or is it nothing still. Gordon takes
all fourteen lines on consignment,
puts them on an upper shelf
near compound miter saws,
two rows up from drills.
He refuses any better placement,
cites little rhyme, no refrain.
On impulse, I buy a worn-out Kirby cheap
to vacuum up the rain.

>   (published by **Jeopardy**; republished
>   by **Thick With Conviction**; *Mapping water*)

Plotting shadows from the chaos
(with a nod to Alex Vouri)

I see none at noon,
long ones crimson
as day dies in the Pacific.

Dead lives turned upright side.
From dusk it's clear
what we cast upon the earth —

no seeds, no water, no light.
Just cacophony slipping through smoke,
half a million ghosts

etched in cinders by a new moon,
grid of darkness, spreadsheet nonpareil.
Or hawks cutting ovals in midnight sky,

mountains askew, smashed by clouds;
oceans, powdered; glaciers on fire;
fires, iced. Pattern that marks the present

in black, turns history into a bell curve —
chart of mistakes ripe for awards,
say, holocaust without equal

or nuclear war of note.
Best tyrant,
dead children with most bloat.

(published by **Literary Chaos**)

Redemption

It's the proper time to absolve your white self
for cruelty to Blackfeet neighbors, hatred

of their casinos, contempt for lodges of sweat.
Lie on Montana railroad tracks

between steel bars laid end to end —
parallels as a kid you placed nickels on

then hid until the train thundered past,
fearful coins would cause derailment,

send boxcars grinding down cinder slopes,
smash you in the trees. Instead, they flattened

nickels until buffalo disappeared, Indian heads
became faint. Clacked on their way, left you

hopeful the conductor would be welcomed
by his kids, pray with them before bed.

Now lie silent, invisible, concave,
arms at your sides, breath held in, head turned

as you listen for the midnight train.
If all the cars click past —

if no rods or cables drag low,
suddenly you are in dark, alone,

stars again above, only crickets clicking —
you will be redeemed, free to rise, renewed,

feel whiteness is goodness, attend
alabaster church, worship a caramel Jesus,

boast though not a sacrifice, your ordeal
was noble. You will be free

to hate in good conscience
as you wait for the morning train.

   (published by **The Curious Record**)

Side effects may include

hair balls, always wheezing,
sawing Barbie Dolls in pieces,
love of ads, bloody stool,

dining out totally nude, shark attack,
calling everybody dude —
constipation, turning tricks,

mushroom highs, harmless fibs,
severe case of boneless ribs,
no desire for iPod tunes,

staying up to watch Fox News —
lust for imitation crab and squid,
wine cooler inebriation,

breast surgery, cheating mate,
spinached teeth on a date,
always right day or night,

four inches added to penis size,
body odor, mad cow bite,
yen for yams and Spam fillets,

inability to go all the way,
pubic hair that will not curl,
forty weeks at Disney World.

(published by **The Dirty Napkin**)

Smoke follows beauty

Wind skips off drifts of snow,
whips campfire flames to life —
smoke chokes me then shifts
for you. It follows beauty,

I say; you twirl and dance
Montana April camping damp.
Birch twigs crack, snap, burn bright —
then retreat, smolder, hide,

yield to winter not yet thawed.
I am quick, bend low,
puff coals turning back
to black, aglow. Wisps of smoke

search for you, whirling off —
embers left behind turn cold
when a branch of snow
lets go.

>   (published by **Labyrinth**;
>   republished in ***Mapping water***)

Sporadic barbarian
(with a nod to Alex Vouri)

At dawn
a great blue heron
flew into my cage
and shut the door with its beak.
At dusk I devoured hot meat
sizzled dark by charcoal grill.
Blew glowing coals back to life.
Carved thirteen new holes
in your picture with my knife.
All in all,
it was quite a day.

    (published by **Jeopardy**)

Still the only bar in Dixon, Montana
(for Richard Hugo, James Welch and J.D. Reed)

I come here Monday on a whim,
hope to find the barmaid in,
serving insights about death
even if they make no sense —
at least, believe I imagined Hugo

floating down the Flathead, belly up,
empty whiskey glass in hand.
It's nearly fifty years since Welch,
Reed and Dick fished the river out
then stopped to drink this bar out too.

Window signs still shine Budweiser red,
reflect the road at Flathead's edge.
Hugo would like blacktop whooshing past,
new, wide, dark as headstones
poets threw empty whiskey bottles at —

lonely highway to Missoula,
lined by white crosses hung with lilies
sagging plastic in the ditch —
announcing another pilgrim nearly blessed.
Downstream, death — same destination

he took binge drinking trips toward.
Even cattails here drown Flathead brown.
The redhead with Van Winkle comes
straight from Welch's poem, eyes swollen
with regret she never escaped,

found peace, Missoula, or the coast.
Maybe river water grabbed her soul,
said *don't go, please stay,
emulate Richie Gray, Dixon's drunk
who went insane, downed shotgun blast,*

matching Flathead brown with red.
I'm not Montanan anymore, own no guns,
don't paint seatbelts on my shirt
to avoid the law. Dick drinks
with Richie down the road, Welch's spirit

floats on wind in France, at dawn skims
the Rhône. Reed probably died alone,
left this bar graveyard quiet
watching Flathead debris sulk by.
My third bourbon, two short of Hugo,

drowns bad memories first. The rest
go under later. I begin to slur my poets,
think I can drive the redhead wild.
She hangs back in shadows
now deep enough to bury hope.

    (published by **Jeopardy**;
    republished in ***Mapping water***)

Tending nuclear bombs
(with a nod to Bob Duke)

Count up from Hiroshima,
1, 2, 3 — Alconbury, England —

7, 8, 9 — 1957, U.S. Air Force,
you twenty at the time,
no idea what half-life means.

Barbed wire, guard towers,
sentries fenced out, in, you
and the other men put nuclear bombs —
never used — to rest,

pack warhead, nose cone,
four wings, fins,
gloves, then your own clothes,
into barrels stenciled in red —
bomb parts — sealed everything tight.

You learned to watch for Commies
sneaking out of fog
but before being overrun,
should madly dig trenches —
the manual said two feet is enough —
roll barrels in, open or not,

use long poles, ten feet,
push earth across, retreat,
let intruders tramp mounds
red from the heat.
Over fifty years have gone by,

friends, bomb-tenders back then,
have cancer, have died.
Your schedule next week,
two sessions of chemo,

radiation treatment five.
Maroon fog creeps in
on little atomic feet —

you count down from 100,
certain to find sleep.

    (published by **The Curious Record**)

Text message from the nursing home

i drool a lot
know if my bdpan is full
see ol geezrs by me die

my kids say they r busy
so i vue lots on tv
fox news, opra, ways to sta yung

they promis food soon
i hope for peas
i will crush thm with my spoon

    (earlier nersion published by **Words-Myth:**
    A Quarterly Poetry Journal)

Vacuuming your cat

Begin with a long hose,
canister in closet, door nearly closed.
Overcoming suspicion takes time.
Use a nozzle meant for blinds,

bristles black like Hitler's hair.
Or don't. Your hose alone
will scare her. Sidle up

as if searching for a spot
to wash yourself in morning sun.
The hose will appear more normal.
Pet her side with a free hand.

The vacuum should be running.
Sneak in a single stroke
with the Hitler wand. But only one.

If the cat remains, watch her tail.
Swishing may mean trouble.
Repeat daily even if it rains.
Pretend to be looking for a place

to stash your hose for good.
Consider yourself lucky if she is fooled.
Keep at it, without variation.

Remember, Darwin had no clue
as to why cats hate vacuums.
After a week, you may break through.
If so, stroke both her sides,

maybe tail. But, do not vacuum ears.
And, don't misread your cat's purr.
We all have growls for things we fear.

> (earlier version published by **Jeopardy**;
> republished by **Tipton Poetry Journal;**
> *Mapping water*)

Early Pilgrim, reluctant cowboy

Poems arranged alphabetically by year:

    1990-99 pages 363-378
    1980-89 pages 379-400
    pre-1980 pages 401-410

Poems 1990-99

At Nez Perce camp with Spirit Woman

Tipi lodge poles point to sky,
random clouds laid on blue like their camp
dotting meadow grass, not as green
though as your eyes. We two see
where Rainbow Warrior fell,

suspect blood brother Five Wounds died
later that day laying siege
to soldiers huddled in hollows so deep
only more Nez Perce blood
could make them rise to fight.

We wander together reviewing death,
see where Wahlitits and wife
lay in final embrace, her birthing day
denied by this battle Chief Joseph
could not defer. You sense her spirit still,

see it bend meadow grass turned gold,
quickly gather red clover
for power before evening sky gone gray.
As for me, I scan the horizon,
wondering why she had no name.

>(published by **Trestle Creek Review**;
>republished by **Poetrymagazine.com**;
>**Labyrinth**)

Belly up
(for Omar Castaneda)

"I ask him if the sky is more blue and the sun
more yellow because those are the colors
we all become when we die."
— Sherman Alexie
in ***The Lone Ranger and
Tonto Fistfight in Heaven***

We must lie white
in sun
hoping to turn tawny
like brothers, sisters
we steal birch, streams
and salmon from.
We must lie without hope
hoping
we will become golden,
cloak shame, feel
genuine sorrow,
bronze our souls.
Being white
we must lie.

(published by **Jeopardy**;
republished in ***Mapping water***)

Burning to no

You've chosen cremation, phoned home,
even faxed your broker,
cc'd those who care and some

who don't. This choice embodies
Pascal's Gamble the sequel —
calculated risk, final effort

to outflank the grim reaper.
Your decision — burn here on Earth,
make hell redundant —

is a chance worth taking,
eclipses coffin wait,
takes the breath away.

But it's no bed of coals out there —
red, or white — no wannabe pyre,
no box seat under night sky.

Of all people, who'd believe
you'd have fierce faith, vision to choose,
certainty the sun will burn out too?

    (published by **Trestle Creek Review**)

Day after reading Raymond Carver's "Late Fragment"

When poets ask,
did you get enough from life,
I too say

yes.
Say my days were filled
watching you patter about the kitchen

up to your cheeks in flour,
Russian teacakes
beginning to form neat rows

on the cookie tray.
It was enough
to sip coffee, watch you

wipe flour on your hip pockets,
sun sweeping the room,
black jeans transformed

amid fine haze
sifting to the floor
where you slid,

making designs,
not rows, but some new dance
I could emulate

if I had time, flour and faith
enough. The cakes took shape,
mounded

like Jupiterean moons
in some galactic oven.
Becoming full, radiating heat

from their whiteness.
It was then
I sensed warmth in the haze.

   (published by **Trestle Creek Review**)

Death by chocolate

Once feeders at brie licks,
now over the edge,
they camp out
near Fudge Kitchen, kill time
baking brownies, eat
the whole panful, watch
Wee Willie Wonka replays,
pray for Valentine's Day year-round.
For kicks they beat each other
with chocolate chip nightsticks.
The more fanatic bite
lenses off malted cameras, gulp down
devil's food subpoenas,
throw Hershey's Kisses to the crowd.
Their mouths gaping, tongues and uvulas
coated dark brown,
they become chocolate undertakers
licensed to mousse.

   (published by **Trestle Creek Review**)

Goodbye to Dad
(with a nod to Gretel Erlich)

Now it is time
for you to fish again. Our breath
catches at each thought of you,
becomes a spring breeze
pushing aside winter, timidly re-greeting
tumbling creek and sun. Can we too
cast furiously, arc tears
and dreams across this blue stream,
tempt you to rise,
whirl skyward, spiral
toward Montana mountains in ragged wind?

Someday we will toast the end
of loneliness, won't really believe then
it can come true.
Nothing has prepared us
for a connection gone so deep
into rainbowed loss. Still, it seems
a premonition of something more
to come — maybe the final calm
we too will feel
after we put our creels in order.

>   (published in Ned Pilgrim's funeral program;
>   different version, "Creels in order," published
>   in 2016 in ***Mapping water***)

If I should blow out

this candle
tenuous as it is
provide assistance in fading
from flame
to pungent smoke —
if I should
in one whispered breath
create passage
from heat
to coolness, glow
to night
I ask
you not assign
guilt
or blame. Know
I could not bear
to see, to feel
the flame
die
on its own.
It was, after all,
my only source of light.

    (published by **Trestle Creek Review**)

Instrument of surrender: Breaking it off at the Little Bighorn Battlefield

Sioux warriors stopped
Yellow Hair here,
cut off
retreat to the river,

forced him back
to the breaks
and death.
We walk, not touching,

past a quiver of graves.
Bailey, the others, here.
Custer, alone,
there. They made a stand

on high ground.
Not high enough really.
You examine surrounding hills,
point out alabaster clusters,

tombstones huddled together
white
amid grass turned brown
by August sun.

You wander off,
distracted,
examine a grave.
I follow, decide not

to recount Sioux tactics,
futile victory
won over a century ago.
Was it last night

under Montana stars plentiful
as sparks from Sioux fires
we decided love
had floated into the night,

drifted
with smoke toward the stars?
By such a fire
Crazy Horse knew

Sioux had a chance,
believed
the next day would be filled
with scalps, most

more gold than red
in the setting sun.
Bleached headstones you admire
reflect the light.

I scan far riverbank,
hope to see
the dead
reclaiming life in the trees.

    (accepted by **Seattle Review**)

In which he blames her infidelity on a throw-away society

My heart drops
down
when I see the crescent moon
unhook herself
from a covey of clouds,
pause in false fullness,
then glide blithely
after others
flitting by

on the far side of the night.
You are the moon.
You move
brightly — lover to lover
then another,
eager
to spend your lifetime
using up
the entire sky.

(published by **Trestle Creek Review**)

Poem not without sound bites

I knew the end
was near, saw a thousand points
of light, stood alone at break
of day, radical dude,
lost soul,
vituperative poet
realizing the fat lady had sung —
or hadn't, but at least had gone down
in a blaze of glory.

I suspected at long last
my love of corporate headquarters or language
was not unblemished, pure as driven snow,
true. I broke the mold, dared to stop
drug abuse, took a fork in the road,
went my own way, finally abandoned
stock options, poetry,
said *where's the beef,*
don't call me,

I'll call you.
I sobbed, yes, uncontrollably,
lacked the right stuff, couldn't pledge
allegiance to flag, Founding Fathers,
CDs, failed to screw you
and the horse you rode in on,
was no Jack Kennedy,
didn't inhale, in fact, sang
Polly Wolly Doodle all the day.

My hope of hopes,
rap music, was on the wane
so I got a life, took a mistress
to write home about —
greeting cards —
final shot at salvation, last chance
for a wonderful life.
Yes, I finally bit my bullet,
turned flushed cheeks to the light.

>(published by **Critical Perspectives on Accounting**)

Poet grants absolution to novelist

It is ok to dream
your balls are big. Huge
in fact. Swinging from side
to side. Pealing so wildly
church steeples cannot support them.
They crash down on the chapel,
crush sinners acting meek
in prayer. You must burn bright candles
in your navel. Cleanse
any sign of guilt. May your prose
smolder from the ordeal.

>(accepted by **Trestle Creek Review**;
>different version published by **Jeopardy**)

Seduced by metaphor

"She was with him again, a heartbeat unbroken,
where time subsided into dawn, and the sunset
gave way to the stars, wheeling across the night."
— Leslie Marmon Silko
in ***Ceremony***

Ceremony has a way of taking hold.
I should have closed my eyes
one more time, imagined

your story arriving, ember arcing
across evening sky —
siren moving above me,

melodic chant making stars unwhirl.
Maybe recited an old invocation,
brought back ancient night,

campfire purple at dusk
again casting your shadow
on the full moon.

I should have told of a goddess of hope,
accepted all her rituals,
kindled, new.

Ceremony has a way of taking hold.
I should have created a tale
with fire in your eyes becoming you.

(published by **Jeopardy**; republished by **Thick With Conviction**; Poetrymagazine.com; **Bellingham Herald**; ***Mapping water***)

**Supposing he had been invited
to the Donner Party**

Not exactly ocean cruise
or get-away flight. No destination resort.
More like a progressive dinner.
Bring prairie schooner,
food. RSVP by late June.

Another California bash, no doubt.
Wagon train en masse mountains to coast,
Big Dipper tipped back so far
all night runs out,

all hope too.
Scoop deep in the main course,
broth, soup, stew.

Near dawn, stars gone,
eat your friend last.

She is delicious.

    (published by **Trestle Creek Review**)

To Exxon a year later

You brought new meaning
to robber baron.
Taught us how to stare
cold as breath on tundra,
pump frozen sod primed with promises
even Arctic fox knew

were lies. Your sleek mukluks
gave you away. Told us
pipeline, tankers,
attorneys slapping our backs in bars,
buying free drinks,
all would bring

sadness
even dutiful glaciers couldn't scrub
away. We followed
your flowing tracks — our backs
to the rising sun, itself giving way
to night — tromped black ice,

piled oily otters, seals,
terns, cheek-high, set them ablaze,
watched the pyre outshine frosty dusk.
Our breath froze white
on the darkened beach. That night
we burned ice to stay warm.

>(published by **Trestle Creek Review**;
>republished by **Canary**; *Mapping water;*
>segments of this poem appear in "To Exxon
>30 years later," and "Slick — to Exxon then
>and BP now")

Poems 1980-89

Angle of repose

It is only by degrees
we arrived at love's central core.
One by one, like layered loam

scraped off bedrock
ready to support
some institution's graying weight,

we peeled lesser habits away.
Showering together was first to go —
your breasts streaking my chest,

mouth nuzzling lips,
spray erasing suds
I'd laid on your chin

with one bubbled stroke.
Late-night dinners went —
Bach swirling amid candled shadows,

your head snuggling in crook
of chin and throat,
our humming moistened by Bordeaux,

dual notes drifting mixed
amid concerto wafting upward
cooling in waxened smoke.

Sleepy hours together turned fetal
became hug of knees —
no more pressing for warmth,

nose resting against neck
as breath ebbed and flowed
in perfumed hair,

thighs molded to derrière —
instead, one morning caress
final layer removed

yielding granite for our love
together. At last
we had a fine foundation to build on.

>(published by **Trestle Creek Review**;
>republished in ***Idaho's Poetry: A
>Centennial Anthology; Mapping water***)

Birches: the father seeks absolution
(for Kamie)

Would half a lifetime of mistakes,
forty years of poor choices, be too much
to forgive? Perhaps ten thousand *No's*,
thick bark cover driven

by paddle-gripping need
gained generations before?
Consider stinging stares,
finger-waving scowls

replete with lectures, all these standing
tall, ponderosa pines
not bending to your need
merely for my love? And punishment,

rules rigid, relentless storm
uprooting birches,
crashing them to forest floor?
Could these ever be absolved?

If you knew my tears squeezed back
longer than exile to crib,
high chair, darkened room,
could you begin to waver?

If you knew my remorse,
tousled hair, hugs — denied,
would you bring forth
some forgiveness, some pardoning,

some swaying of ponderosa strength
you now embody?
In short
if I with rope and tackle

located one uprooted birch,
pale bark rotting,
if I rigged pulleys with hemp
around scarred sides,

began pulling, sweating, straining
to hoist it majestic,
would you —
if not preoccupied with standing tall

in well-learned sternness —
would you dip down,
take rope, pull with me,
hearts open,

believing together
forest of ponderosas
would become lithe birches, swaying,
together bending low?

    (accepted by **Trestle Creek Review**)

Catch-22 in Northern Idaho

"White supremacists were denied a cross-burning
permit today because of tinder-like conditions
in the Hayden Lake area."
                              — Seattle Times

It was not my heat
alone or yours saying
in Nazi breezes
scoop up one white cat
clutch fur to chest
have for an instant
a monogrammed Yosserian coat
holding the very entrails in.
Soon purrs turned low to growls
claws stitching black reminders
saying I couldn't have you
in the holding
or the setting free.

    (published by **Trestle Creek Review**)

Coeur d'Alene spring: Reliving his regret for the 23rd time

So begins another dusk, red sun
dipping below darkened sill,
departure, like yours, summoning
dim memory, lyric poem,

"The Pasture," Frost's account
of love dancing in me now,
partner to fading rays. I recall
New England speaker shy to lover

probably summer blonde
like you glistening tawny
in sun-streaked open pose,
I'm going to clean the pasture spring,

rake leaves away, maybe
linger as cloudy water clears;
I shan't be gone long. You come too.
He planned to fetch a calf so young

it tottered under mother's lick
the way your shivers quicken
when I nuzzle kisses up your sides.
You come too, he whispered a second time.

I wonder if lover seized that chance
took outstretched hand
for one hour left tedious chores
behind, tromped arm and waist

with him away together
spongy meadow grass imprinting love
as they strolled, two yet one
passing afternoon under shadowed willows

glistening white. Or did she too
allow burdens, not quite trivial
not yet mundane, to clog spring again,
choke pasture grass, say, *Sorry,*

much to do before summer comes?
I hope he smiled, knew muddied water
bawling calf, meadow also waited
tending. I hope he managed

one more *Won't you come too?*
just before the leaving.

    (published by **Trestle Creek Review**)

Conspiracy of vegetarians

Before we raid the salad bar,
we must plan how to avoid

gun emplacements, bunkers,
camouflaged snipers lying in wait

among moist onions. As dawn comes
rebellion red, we'll swoop down,

zigzag through the cafeteria, sweep past
that damned fifty-cents-an-ounce sign,

outflank troops waiting to behead
those daring to sneak an olive in

before they reach the scale.
Havoc-wreakers of three-bean salad,

we'll pillage cowering bowls of lettuce,
plunder carrot trays, take

the most slender bread sticks hostage.
It is then we'll ride off,

marauders splashing wild through pools
of blue cheese and Italian dressing,

dragging bean sprouts behind us. Yes,
we'll finally have our way with broccoli.

(published by **Trestle Creek Review**)

**Cuddly Bear snares
the Copenhagen beauty**
(with a nod to Paul Bair and Barry Baker)

Her skin whipped Indian brown
by Montana wind
cries *free me* to faded Levis,
almost escapes, thighs gone wild.
Little Bear, cuddly
beyond his nineteen years, sees love
nestled deep in tight jeans

taut blouse — tobacco-filled cheek.
He, also hip-pocket-white-ring
shouting Copenhagen to the stars, knows
she sways smiling
not because cowboys grin
shy at her red hair,

green eyes. Not because drunks
stagger past, caressing,
round, riveted cheeks,
heavy hands probing.
But yes because she too knows
before Missoula night
slips by, before Big Dipper retreats

from rodeo dawn, before winds rise
bronc-riding warm,
her brown breath will ooze,
swirl with bear breath,
both panting home the stars.
And Cuddly Bear, brown eyes, brown teeth

flashing as he blows juice
straight and true,
knows let-me-go moans,
jeans, tanned cheeks
will be his by dawn, will become
snoose-covered love
spitting out the sky.

   (published by **Trestle Creek Review**)

In which he accepts the feminist point of view

Geese sweep past in blackness,
vee their driven way north,
forms outlined gray
against the full moon.
I am certain it must be
a female who veers
off, fights her solitary way
up the gaggle's ragged edge,
takes her turn in the lead.
She slices night sky
with fresh fierceness.
We tromp wet beach together.
I sink barefoot,
filling your tracks in the sand.

   (published by **Trestle Creek Review**)

Ketchum, Idaho:
At the Hemingway Memorial

Corner tavern, call it Slavey's.
Jami — with an *i* — barmaid
eight weeks now, going on nine,
waves you up this canyon — Sun Valley,
where women, forty, sweatered tight,
lure wanderers, eyes ablaze,

to condos October brown,
autumn sunlight going
down. Here, Paul Anka,
no longer crooning
Fifties tunes,
hums lullabies to night.

Here, Sun Valley carpets
red as your eyes
soak up old men,
themselves absorbing winks
barmaids serve, fondling
pointed invitations

before fatigue sets in,
taking them petrified to sleep.
Lives here all wheeze
as one, mostly for young breasts —
breasts that wives, naked
near Anka's place, also moan for.

Here, flames consume cottonwood,
itself dead since Hemingway blasted out
his brains another lost generation ago,

Idaho's only genius,
flowing dark crimson
to death, fomentation, peace,

union — vivid testimony
to Ketchum's insane games.
One mile beyond Sun Valley, above
lovers gone cottonwood bad,
his bronze bust, cloaked purple now
by mountain shadows, guards

some faded plaque, inscription saying
he dearly loved high, blue,
windless skies. You, here, like him,
in wind — clouds slipping pink
to black — grip no gun, lack brilliance,
have no courage to greet death.

Can breasts, even Jami's, rising
to meet night, or old ones
dying in time to fire,
keep you wandering, searching
for meaning, not just Sun Valley's,
but meaning Hemingway gave up on

when he squeezed away his life?
Or will you hobble hills to senility,
watch mates take their place
in the valley, outglow embers,
moan away Ketchum nights, as you doze,
tightening your grip on the sky?

(earlier version published by **Trestle Creek Review**)

Late autumn run beside Lake Fernan

Rippling waves flow in, out;
each moist breath comes fast
then goes, so I pant
happy to be striding strong,
Fernan's green surface
lapping at my side.
I wish you, your slender thighs here

to match me breath for breath
sway for sway.
In my moss-fringed race,
shadow dancing gray
to green, I accede to the rhythm,
pound again repeating
a solitary plea:

come run these
miles at water's edge,
lope each spongy trail, come
surge like clouds
painting shadows across this path.
But soggy footprints
shouting *runner* to applauding rain,

pulsing waves,
even these know
no lithe companion, no curving shadow
of hips and breasts
drift across moss or lake
blow in, mingle,
brief breeze rushing past in mist,

another lip-swollen escape.
How is it such a scenario —
lake to waiting moss,
ten miles of green on green —
is replayed with each breath
in runner's stride
no matter my pace, no matter

what effort I expend
to envision your form beside?
Perhaps like wind
chasing beleaguered clouds, someday
I'll flow your shadow's edge
finally stop reprieves
promised with each step

and breath. Until then my crazy lungs
will frost the October sky.

    (published by **Trestle Creek Review**)

Phoning from the ant farm aisle at Spokane Pets

I'm watching them half-envious, lover.
Ants dutifully bury their dead,
grieve quickly, then return still working,
the ceremony almost too brief.

They carry on. Crawl caved-in lives.
Lug loads thirty times their weight
through sandy passages dreary
as Seattle winter. Sometimes

two of them meet, caress
each other in darkness,
tap out a lack of space,
make their ways past

in tunnel freshly dug,
being oh so careful
not to prolong
any touch — then hurry on,

gloomy lifers without reprieve.
Forgive such babbling,
love. I really called to say
only three more stops —

two out east, one at the mall.
Keep your candlelight soft,
your wine red, warm. We'll lie together,
kissing all night in the hall.

    (published by **Trestle Creek Review**;
    different version, "Text from the exotic pets store,"
    published in 2020 by **Tipton Poetry Journal**)

Poet's crossing at Pillar Point

You make your choice by choosing you.
In half light, not white, not gray
your own castaway grips one oar
itself lashed tight to open boat
trapped by strait and rocky shore.
No easy choice, this one of foam

waves tipping white, milked-out coast —
alabaster dashed on stone.
Pulse thumps time to brine, to spray.
Steers its own circuitous route.
Drunken critics stagger bluffs,
note milky struggle, cheer your craft

spinning mad outside the surf. They
don't know it's you, but if they do
prefer Juan de Fucan wind
to foundered dinghy, one choked oar.
Circle widening, white wake in foam
choice or choosing — surf or stone.

(published by **Quaint Canoe**)

Pre-dawn vigil at Kootenai Medical Center
(for John)

> "Son, thou are ever with me, and all that I have is thine."
> — Luke 15:31

My only son lies unconscious,
tubes dripping hope into cheeks
flushed ruby by I.V. flow. I see

last summer's campfire we two
blew to life in meadow dusk,
anglers' attempt to keep Montana cold

from freezing fingers off our fished-out hands.
Today's trip testing Priest Lake alone
netted his limit of poison,

not nearly as much fun as bringing in
three cutthroat now untended,
glass-eyed beside the vacant boat.

I wish for Montana twilight, we both
shivering back the day's rainbows
eager fighters jumping against the sky,

fierce competitors for Royal Coachmen
arced toward their stream —
invitation to exchange

icy creek for burlap creel.
Night flames took crackling hold,
licked lodge pole twigs gray with age.

I roughed his hair, brushed fire-red cheeks,
let loose laughter that followed ash
to coolness in the floating smoke.

His chest rises, dives deep
in this struggle to keep life.
I hook his hand in mine,

squeeze and release with each faint breath.
At times I see sparks
sputtering against the night sky.

>(published by **Trestle Creek Review**;
>republished in ***Idaho's Poets: A
>Centennial Anthology***; ***Mapping water***)

Ruling out indictment

Now that I also cook
even if only limp linguini,
wash sullen dishes

while you dry,
wiping away teary streaks
steamy, dripping china clean,

permit me
to lay down one condition,
a single setting

of this our equal pact.
When you and I,
buzzing here, there, in,

out, ever spinning wild
days away,
alone,

finally land unchipped,
still dizzy from the whirling,
home,

let us press together
like droplets on that moist bowl
not letting life's careening

wipe away
such tenderness as does your towel
one final bead,

itself clinging precariously
to the lip
of our tenuous dish.

> (published by **Trestle Creek Review**;
> republished in ***Mapping water***;
> different version, "Vow" published in 2013
> by **Kumquat Poetry Challenge**)

Student loan repayment time

Hello, I'm here from Payco —
my company sends you greetings;
we wish you well but need
your cash. A bank back East,
or was it L.A.,

tired of endless excuses, said
*oh too bad you can't meet
obligations*, didn't care
one bit for sick children —
in short, didn't believe

you have no dough.
So Payco, your loving, loaning friend,
bought your debt, believes
in you, knows you have means
to pay and pay. I'm here

to convey our care —
but my U-Haul truck is here
(in case you don't love back)
to move your life away,
along with car and sofa if cash

isn't in this sack
by yesterday.
Don't try tears to wash ink
incurred by college
from this note. You must yield

before you feed or clothe your kids.
That can wait.
As for me, I'd like
your boat, your bed,
even you if I find it in the print.

Of course, right here
it says *one slender lovely,
complete with hazel eyes
and pointy breasts*. Too bad.
I'll be gentle, but remember,

even taut nipples won't stay
next month's payment.
I'll be back for silver,
curtains, towels, dishes —
yes, even panties in the drawer.

    (published by **Trestle Creek Review**)

Poems pre-1980

Born of man

Born of man, born of man helpless.
Brought forth from death
to suffer life.
Hippies beckon. Black men revolt.
We want out.
Parents deaf cannot find time ... time.
A man born a mound of clay,
shaped in the image of violence,
reared in hate —
but he was such a good boy.
Exposed from the first
to hours of muck, to minutes of love;
ten roads stretch out,
yet one leads right.
Figures in the dark...
a flick of a knife ...
bomb blasts black church ...
all hell broke loose ...
youth saves drowning child —
for a rich, full life?
Goodness is there —
there to be fought for,
there to be grasped,
and there to be won.
A man who wins goodness,
who struggles for truth,
for honesty, for justice,
who would sacrifice life
for ideals he believes in;

this man who wins goodness,
this man of courage,
this man to esteem —
also the man who wins grace.

(published by **The Muse**)

Face the muse-ic 1

Tell of wily Red Eye, Muse,
and if he stands on rock or sand.
Is the mask from which he peers
concealing more than mortal name?
Does this critic match the wit
and ideals of we who stand
alone to take the brutal blows
for words we turn into mistakes?
Does air that whistles from his words
blow thoughts of hatred through our minds,
or will we listen, nod and turn
to walk away, the truth to find?

Mortal, mortal, do I detect
a wisp of wonder for he who hides
behind the mask of one Red Eye?
It's true that blurred his vision is
when through a mask he tries to stare
and then to rip at all in view.
Not called reform or criticism,
but a yearning of the mind,
is the single sheet of feeling
published when the urge is nigh.
Heed not the words of stinging passion,
for in time they will have died.
Quickly memories of Red Eye
reach their peak and then subside.

>(sample of a series of 11 poetic columns
> accepted and/or published by **Wescolite**,
> newspaper at Western Montana College)

Face the muse-ic 2

What of our state of mind, O Muse,
and why do we of a nation great
not see or sense our obvious fate —
the end that comes from pessimism
and nothing more than criticism?
The people stand with outstretched hand
and shove and push across the land
yet do not see the hour glass sand
is running out and soon will be
draining away to eternity.

Mortal, mortal, your look of gloom,
though not unjust and wholly wrong,
is aimed at but the lowly throng,
not at ones who wise will be
enough to keep your country free —
but given time, the dawn you'll see.
It's true that some could never care,
could never rise to meet the dare,
would help their country not, yet cry
for aid and welfare until they die.
But most put on the yoke of toil
and to their country are ever loyal.
These people of strength will stand up tall
and by the fates shall never fall.

> (sample of a series of 11 poetic columns
> accepted and/or published by **Wescolite**,
> newspaper at Western Montana College)

Memories of Ski Gulch

Now that gold seems free,
elusive flakes we panned
lay glittering in my mind.
Hoarded nuggets seeking love.

Water carrying wealth
to a miner's pouch still flows,
but aspen groves of guilt
won't let gold fever finally die.

Someday I'll trudge your sides
again, bring shiny bits
floating to the surface. Then,
tell me buttery metal we panned
was made for tempting fools.

(published in *National Anthology of Poetry*)

Retort

You dare skulk in here,
hate running off like tallow,
asking my forgiveness.

Take your whimpering fears,
your trembling ways of pleading.
Lick your wounded ego
and turn and face the wall.

> (published in ***National Anthology of Poetry***)

Teacher bigot

You stand there fat
and smirking, gleefully

forcing us to eat
your idiotic drippings.

Think we are hungry.
Why not smash our faces,

and toothless, enjoy our gurgling
beneath your bloody boot?

> (published in ***National Poetry Anthology***)

Walls of wisdom

Within the walls of wisdom
will I take my stand, or
over the fences of learning

to knowledge shall I flee?
On endless shores of experience
I will spend my days,

until the hand of death
shall grasp me, clutch me, pull me down
and leave my years of searching

lying in the sand.
I sought truth and beauty,
leaving always ignorance

upended in my wake.
As I learned and laughed and knew,
the last frontier of knowing loomed

clear within my view.
Insight was the rusty key
that turned the lock in future's door,

that brought together grains of wisdom
within the hourglass —
trapped inside by fleeting time

to struggle in the dark.
Until the false should sink below,
then slowly slip away.

I learned what man was thinking,
what he was dreaming of;
I glimpsed the fate of nations

and what they did not heed;
all there was to know and learn,
everything I saw,

but then the glass of time
ran out, and I was there —
no more.

    (accepted by **The Muse**)

The woods near our home

In the woods near our home, we hear
the gentle drops of rain,
through the trees.
Just a soft pad passing leaves
though it sounds like many feet.
The leaves fall gently too in those woods
near our home.
The wind blows cool, oh so cool,
and the stream runs away refreshing,
so refreshing.

>   (*Pilgrim's first poem*, earlier version
>   published in **This is my life**, sixth-grade
>   booklet, Bagley School, Dillon, Mont.)

Index of poem titles

Titles are alphabetized by the first major word, followed by the page number in this volume.

300 streams of memory, 245
Accidental dawn, 273
A few obscene words escape, 3
Afghanistan misery index, 131
Aftermath, 274
After the falls, 132
After the kill, 59
Angle of repose, 379
Airport security, 246
All quiet on the Iraqi front, 309
Almost, 91
Always speaking truth
  to power, 133
America, 2019, 33
Anemic epiphany, 275
Anemone, 221
Angle of repose, 379
Another Bellingham
  Valentine's Day, 167
Antique store mannequin, 4
At the Aryan Nations cross
  burning, 276
At the Kootenai High School
  homecoming, 277
At the Nez Perce camp
  with Spirit Woman, 363
At the Vietnam Memorial, 5
Attuned to home, 168
At White House Ruins, 278
Bakery, 60
Bain Marie, 279
Bats at the hummingbird
  feeder, 310
Beginning of forgetting, 92
Bellingham Caesar, 193
Bellingham limerick, 168
Belly up, 364

Benchmark, 93
Bible tweet, 34
Birches: the father seeks
  absolution, 381
The bitter end, 133
Bituminous nightmare, 169
Blueprint, 6
Books on the way out, 94
Born of man, 401
Brautigan breakfast, 34
Breathing lesson, 247
Breathing snow, 222
Brush with godliness, 280
Burning to no, 365
Cairn, 96
Cairnly power, 97
Call waiting, 98
Candle rescue, 194
Can you kill a priest with a 1-iron
  if you keep your head down, 281
The capes we wear, 7
Capital love, 170
Card from Montana, only snow
  on the cover, 134
Cast away at Larrabee Beach, 223
Catch-22 in Northern Idaho, 383
Cell phone dolor at SeaTac
  airport, 333
Centered, 98
Centering, 224
Chicken, 311
Choosing a nickname
  for Jesus, 249
Choppy water, 250
Claiming, not owning, 135
Coeur d'Alene spring: Reliving
  his regret for the 23rd time, 384
Congratulations on your breast
  implants, 252
Conspiracy of vegetarians, 386
Count ravens, 282

Covert rainbow, 8
Cuddly Bear snares
  the Copenhagen beauty, 387
Damp dance, 99
Dark migration, 283
Dashboard savior, 253
Day after reading Raymond
  Carver's "Late fragment," 366
Day of beckoning, 284
The deadhover, 61
Death by chocolate, 367
Deep end, 334
Defense for mailing
  panties back, 336
Déjà vu tridundancy, 35
Deserted advice, 311
Destined to rhyme, 337
Diagramming love, 136
Doing crank, 338
Doing nothing wrong and
  still losing, 285
Door, 62
Dream back, 36
Dreaming on key, 136
Dregs, 195
Drying tear, sullen sky, 137
Dweeb scarfs down yellow thing
  on a stick, 225
Eclectic suitcase, 9
Editing your life, 312
Embers, 10
The end, 225
Erasing black, 63
Erratic tears, 64
Eternal life, 313
Etiquette lesson, 65
Evading gray, 11
Executive orders, 100
Exhalation, 254
Existential diagram, 101
Existential haircut, 102

Exploding mosquitos, 196
Expect no rescue from a Cyclops
  with delicate hands, 255
Fab Four failure, 197
Face the muse-ic 1, 403
Face the muse-ic 2, 404
Faint memories of a beekeeper's
  daughter, 226
Fake dreams, 138
Fake nudes, 37
Family of widows, 139
Fencing in darkness, 314
Final blizzard, 67
Final say, 140
Finally talking to a guru
  in India, 141
Financial planning session, 339
Fire licks the canyon rim, 198
First sign of wind, 103
Fitting end, 68
Flat-line, 69
Fluke, 171
Forced feeding, 199
Fragile X parent, 315
Fresh graves in black sand, 340
Full creel at sunset, 199
Full of yourself, 103
Gravity of the situation, 286
Gerunds running down
  my leg, 227
Gestapo glaciers, 200
Getting even, 13
Gettysburg tweet, 172
God walks out of math
  proficiency exam, 70
Going south, 256
Gone to rubble, 104
Goodbye to dad, 368
Gourmet, 316
Gravity of the situation, 286
Grim reaper, 228

Half lithe, 142
Hawking holy books, 200
Headboard, 317
The heaped wheel barrow, 318
Hear no evil, 341
Higgs Boson particle, 229
Hoarding, 230
Holstered, 38
Homage, 143
Homeless night watchman, 105
Hooking black sky, 172
Hope, 257
Hope synchs, 106
Horses, whiskey, ropes, 201
Hot, 201
The hum, 39
I cannot do the splits, 173
Ice caving, 287
I eat bitter hearts, 288
If, 319
If a tree falls, 202
If God searches your room, 144
If hope were a shriek
  in the night, 203
If I should blow out, 369
I herded flies, Buzz, when
  I dyed, 320
I miss her more, 71
Imposing intelligence, 289
Inferno, 72
Inflicting scars, 107
In my dream, 289
Instrument of surrender:
  Breaking it off at the Little
  Bighorn Battlefield, 370
Intensely dead, 40
Intertwined whisks, 73
Invisible, 258
In which he accepts the feminist
  point of view, 388
In which he blames her infidelity
  on a throw-away society, 372
In which the romantic writes
  one last poem before
  having a beer, 343
Ironing my face, 321
It is what it was, 41
It's not nothing, 174
John two sixteen, 322
Ken Burns effect, 231
Ketchum, Idaho: At the
  Hemingway Memorial, 389
Knives in ice, 290
La chanson, 14
Laminated, 42
La Push, 43
Last, 15
Last one clapping, 16
Late autumn run beside
  Lake Fernan, 391
Late call from Plato's cave, 291
Late warning, 323
The leaving, 258
Leaving at the break, 73
Left for dead, 259
Letter found on a flash drive
  near the B.C. border, 324
Letter from the Wolong
  Reserve, 175
Let us dream, 17
Lie at a slow pace, 176
Like a fenced-in dog, 14
Life benedict, 204
Light found to have weight, 145
Lilac moon, 177
Little adobe something-or-other
  in Santa Fe, 178
Limerick 1, 146
Limerick 2, 146
Lit exam, 147
Long stumps of hope, 108
The lord's tweet, 148

Love advice, 45
Love that operates, 205
Love you more, 109
Low-tide triage, 14
Lucky, 179
Making cadaver scents, 75
Man pleads guilty in death
   of relationship, 18
Mapping water, 180
Martha's Cafe, 232
The math, 76
Memories of Ski Gulch, 405
Mercy-killing marriage, 206
Miasma, 77
Migratory text. 109
Minoan moment, 234
Missed connections, 292
Missoula migration, 148
Missoula possums, 149
Montana chicken-killing day, 293
Montana condolences,
   of a kind, 110
Montana harvest, 111
Mourning becomes eclectic, 181
My conclusive dance frame, 20
My last professor, 150
My mama's waltz, 46
My only son, 345
Natural orders, 78
Never wrong, 47
New twist on the end, 21
Nibblers, 79
Night-blooming cereus, 182
No absolution, 112
No day to be named
   after a uvula, 113
No design on the sky, 346
No giving up, 183
No leaving, 80
No mending love, 151
No more argument, 81

No more desert, 295
No more robbery, 114
Noose, 295
No release, 115
No way in, 347
Not alone, 235
Not biting, 116
Not still water. 152
Not stomping I LOVE YOU
   in the snow, 82
Note on my windshield, 325
Obsession, 22
Odd, 117
Old poet, 23
On guard, 237
On my gravestone, 238
One-mime town, 207
One thousand seconds, 83
Oregon Coast rainbow
   birthing, 208
Orphan, 208
Out of control, 209
Out of Missoula, 184
Out of Montana, for good, 48
Packing tattoos, 185
Painting lesson, 296
Painting the soul, 260
Panic knot, 84
Parenthetical, 118
Past tents, 153
Pawnshop, 348
Pee hate, 261
Phoning from the ant farm aisle
   at Spokane Pets, 393
Picture please, 297
Please, 119
Plotting romance, 262
Plotting shadows
   from the chaos, 349
Poem not without
   sound bites, 373

Poem to name perfume after, 298
Poem to scrape pelts by, 299
Poet grants absolution
    to novelist, 374
Poet's crossing
    at Pillar Point, 394
Poplars, 84
Posse of angels, 239
Post-cuckold stress syndrome, 301
Powdered water, 50
Pre-dawn vigil at Kootenai
    Medical Center, 395
Primary love, complementary
    colors, 302
Publishing in The New Yorker, 303
Python, 51
Question of humility, 120
Quid pro quo, 240
Rafting with Fitzgerald, 304
Ravel, 121
Reading, 85
Read-out, 121
Real man howls, 154
Recalling fragments, 23
Reciting night sky, 186
Redemption, 350
Red sky at night, 263
Reliving Vietnam at the Dillon,
    Montana class reunion, 210
Reprise for hope, 264
Reprise, of a sort, 52
Rescue mission, 265
Resigning from being messiah, 86
Retort, 406
Revolutions, 155
Richter scale, 326
Roseate, 86
Ruling out indictment, 397
Runner-up disciple, 24
Salt over the left shoulder, 187
Scattering ashes at Squalicum
    Beach, 188

Screw the pretentious poets, 328
Sea change, 122
Second Coming expert, 189
Second person, 156
Seduced by metaphor, 375
Several supple weasels, 87
Shame remains, 53
She-devil, 157
Side effects may include, 352
Silenced night, 158
Six ounces late, 241
Slick — to Exxon then
    and BP now, 330
Smoke follows beauty, 353
Smudging, 242
Solstice ceremony at
    Medicine-walker's, 25
Solstice ceremony near
    Mount Baker, 26
Spiral down, 27
Sponges, 304
Sporadic barbarian, 354
Stick horses, 243
Still glow, 123
Still the only bar in Dixon,
    Montana, 355
Storm, 124
Student loan repayment time, 399
Summer hymn, 124
Summer maid, 190
Supposing he had been invited
    to the Donner Party, 376
SWAG, 266
Swallow, 159
Sweet peace, 125
Table-side magic, 212
Taut too, 159
Teacher bigot, 406
Tending nuclear bombs, 357
Tent not taken, 191
Text from the exotic pets store, 28
Texting the savior, 160

Text message from the nursing home, 358
Things are well and going good, 213
This being America, there were patriots present, 332
Toasting the city of subdued excitement, 214
To Exxon 30 years later, 54
Too Exxon a year later, 377
Too fat to hang, 267
Too much gossamer, 215
Too much hope, 305
Too willing a Montana martyr, 56
Topless woman steals baby Jesus from Vatican nativity scene, 29
Traitor Joe, 192
Trek, 306
Tweet from the third pew, 244
Two dogs, one stick, 268
Unknown clichés, 269
Upgrading to poutine at the Radium, B.C. bar & grill, 161
Use two pillows, sleep fast, 307
Vacuuming your cat, 359
Vacuuming around the dead, 162
Vast silence, 88
Verbal agreement, 270
Violent male rut, 30
Viral in Norway, 126
Viral ending, 31
Walls of wisdom, 407
War memorial, 163
Warning, 216
Wash your hands, 32
Water birthing, 271
Web mutiny, 308
Wedding rescue, 127
Wheelchair warrior, 217
When I went out to hang myself, 89
Who's counting, 128
Wild and scenic aneurysm, 57
The woods near our home, 409
Working with wind at Canyon de Chelly, 129
Wrong a lot, 164
Yellowstone recital, 165
Yes, yes, oh, yes, 218
Zigzag mowing, 218

About the author

Timothy Pilgrim is a native of Montana, where he taught high school English, journalism and speech before leaving to teach college in Idaho, North Carolina, and California. He taught classes in journalism at Western Washington University in Bellingham from the early 1990s until he reired in 2013. He lives there with his wife, author Carolyn Dale.

Pilgrim is one of three poets in **Bellingham Poems** (Flying Trout Press, 2014) and published his first book of poems, **Mapping water** (Flying Trout Press) in 2016. His poems appear in anthologies such as **Idaho's Poets: A Centennial Anthology** (University of Idaho Press), **Weathered Pages: The Poetry Pole** (Blue Begonia Press), and **Tribute to Orpheus 2** (Kearney Street Books).

He received degrees from Western Montana College (B.S., Secondary Education), the University of Montana (M.A., English) and the University of Washington (M.A. and Ph.D., Communications). Among his scholarly writings, he and Dale and authored an editing textbook, **Fearless Editing** (Pearson, 2006, republished, Focal Press, 2015).

Pilgrim enjoys hiking, snow shoeing, fly fishing, and dancing and has run five marathons. He now bicycles, walks and tries to remember to breathe deeply as he practices yoga.

To contact him, email: cairnshadowpress@gmail.com.

www.ingramcontent.com/pod-product-compliance
Lightning Source LLC
Chambersburg PA
CBHW021050080526
44587CB00010B/201